A ENZO

EN TU 1995 CUMPLEAÑOS

CON INMUTABLE AFECTO
DE LA MADRE DE TUS
HIJOS *Rosetta*

12/9/95

MACNO

M A C N O

ANDREA DE CARLO

Translated from the Italian by William Weaver

HARCOURT BRACE JOVANOVICH, PUBLISHERS

SAN DIEGO   NEW YORK   LONDON

Library of Congress Cataloging-in-Publication Data
De Carlo, Andrea, 1952–
Macno.
I. Title.
PQ4864.E236M313   1987   853'.914   86-9864
ISBN 0-15-154899-4

Text Design by Robert Bull
Printed in the United States of America
First edition
A B C D E

To Federico Fellini

It's often said that life is strange.
Oh yes, but compared to what?
STEVE FORBERT

MACNO

O N E

He is on his way back from taping another version of the Third Anniversary speech, which should be broadcast a month and a half from now as if it were being televised live. He is leaning back on the rear seat of the long black automobile, looking for the fourth time at the same section of the tape on the little monitor screen: the gaps in tension, the lapses of tone. He is irritated, depressed, tired; the seat is too enfolding, the automobile too well soundproofed.

He presses the rewind button; he looks outside. The palace guards always have this slow way of recognizing the motorcade. They wait till the other guards, behind the glass panes, press the buttons to open the gates. Then they follow the two wings as they part, and stand at either side of the driveway as if they saw nothing more. The two motorcycles, the great black car, the other pair of motorcycles drive into the park, over the crunching white gravel.

Macno presses the play button, and at that same moment a siren screams. The car stops, swerves, then accelerates. Macno slips to one side; Palmario sprawls on top of him, trying to press him down. But Macno hasn't the slightest desire to be blown to bits without at least getting a look at the person aiming a bazooka at him or drawing the pin of the grenade or. He frees himself from the heavy protective arm, raises his head, looks through the bulletproof glass: security men are cutting across the lawn, running. Somebody fires a volley from a submachine gun; the shots, close by, shatter the air. More sirens start blaring from other points of the park, on different frequencies.

The black automobile concludes its curve along the edge of the park; it brakes at the palace steps. Palmario gets out, runs around the car, opens Macno's door before anyone else can do it. The outriders jump down from their motorcycles, join the palace guards deployed in a fan around the car. Macno gets out, young and dark, agile in his black, Japanese-style suit. He goes to the first step, between two lines of guards; he turns toward the lawn.

The security men are running along the edge of the bamboo grove. There are more shots nearby, and suddenly two green figures emerge from the reeds, rolling on the ground even before the men swarm around them, kicking, as more and more appear, in a second.

Macno leans toward the scene. He says, "There are only two."

"Perhaps," Palmario says, at his side.

Macno comes down one step; he comes down the whole staircase and runs over the white gravel. Palmario dashes after him, and the guards after Palmario. They run over the neatly mowed lawn, in arrowhead formation.

They rush to the tangle of bodies, where it is hard to distinguish the frantic arms and legs and backs. "Take it easy!" Macno shouts. The security men turn around, their movements frozen.

Macno comes forward. He says "Take it easy" again. One after another, the sirens go dead; the air settles down. There is only the gasped breathing, the clatter of buckles and boots and gun barrels. The security men rise to their feet, one after another; they spread out in a semicircle, to allow Macno by.

On the ground there is a heavy man with reddish hair sprawled on his back. He barely raises his head, looking up with little eyes. One eyebrow is reddened; blood trickles from his nose. His green military coverall is torn, revealing a hairy arm; one of his big feet is without a shoe. His chest swells and subsides.

Macno looks at the second person on the ground, and it is a girl, with short blonde hair. She is curled up on her side, her arms folded to protect her head. She is wearing a green coverall like the man's; it is stretched tight at the curve of the hips. Macno looks at one ankle; it is very pale, above a white sock almost without elastic.

3

He turns and says, "There was no need to kill them, for Christ's sake."

The security men draw back half a pace, lowering their eyes. Their officer says, in a murmur, "We couldn't tell if they were armed or not." He points with his chin at the little TV camera on the grass, smashed, a few feet from the girl.

Gradually, the girl lowers her hands, bares her face; leaning on an elbow, she looks up. Her hair is pasted, in clumps, to her forehead; there is a faint scratch on one cheekbone; her pupils are so dilated that her pale eyes seem black. Her lips are trembling, delicately.

Macno bends over her; he says, "I'm very sorry."

She looks at him, sniffs. She sits up, rubbing one knee.

Macno holds out a hand. The security men are panting, motionless, behind him, mingled with the palace guards. Palmario glances around, checking the park.

The girl takes the extended hand and rises to her feet. She tests one leg. She says, "Don't worry, I'm fine." She has a German accent; her tone is even too nonchalant, considering the pallor of her face, with its fine features. She turns and looks to the end of the lawn: the great white palace.

The red-haired guy allows a security man to pull him to his feet. He takes a couple of steps. He shakes his head, touches his nostrils with cautious fingers.

"Why did you come in here?" Macno asks, staring first at him, then at her.

"To film," the girl says. Color is returning to her cheeks; her eyes are very pale again.

"Film what?" Macno, asks.

"You," the girl says. She looks into his eyes for two seconds or three.

With the tip of his foot Macno touches the remains of the little TV camera. He says, "Who for?"

"Nobody," the girl says. She runs a rapid hand through her hair; she says, "We're free-lance."

Macno looks at her full rosy lips; he turns toward the security officer; he says, "Well, maybe we should start really worrying."

The officer is silent for a moment; he says, "They must have climbed over to the west of the gate."

Macno bends down to collect the remains of the camera; he studies it closely, as you might study a small dead animal. He looks up at the pair in green coveralls and says, "We'll have to ship you back to your country. Normally you'd be tried, and all the rest, I believe."

The red-haired guy dissolves in a liquid expression of relief, a fish who's wriggled off the hook. He says, "Thank you, Mr. President."

The girl turns to look at him; she takes a step toward Macno and says, "Wait. We weren't going to film you secretly. We wanted to interview you. We were going to ask you."

Macno hands the destroyed little camera to the officer, who passes it to one of his men. Macno says to the girl, "Don't you know that interviewing me is very complicated? You can't just turn up at the gate with a camera."

"I know," the girl says. "That's why we climbed over."

The red-haired guy looks at her with alarmed eyes; the security men sway on their legs; Palmario looks at Macno.

For a moment Macno hesitates between different words;

5

he tilts his head. He says to the girl, "What's your name?"

"Lise Förster," the girl says. There is a distrustful and ironic glint in her eyes, behind the shock and the uncertainty of the situation.

Macno says, "All right, Lise. Since you're so incredibly shameless, and the security here works so badly, I'll grant you that interview."

The girl draws back just a little. She says, "Thanks."

Macno addresses the red-haired guy; he says to him, "And what's your name?"

"Ted Wesley, Mr. President," the red-haired guy says with an American accent. He says, "I'm the cameraman, Mr. President."

"You'll stay, too, naturally," Macno says. "You're both my guests, here in the palace."

The red-haired cameraman has a hard time getting out words; he says, "Thank you, Mr. President."

"Not at all," Macno says. "And in this country they call me just Macno, Mr. Wesley." He says "Good afternoon," turns; the security men step aside to let him pass.

The red-haired cameraman scratches his head; he looks at the blonde girl only when Macno is a hundred paces off, at least.

T W O

Lise flings the covers aside and gets out of bed. She goes to the window, pulls open the curtain; light spurts into the room, and the walls fade from dark blue to pale azure. She presses her nose to the pane, looks outside: the rear half of the park spreads all the way to the distant line of the wall. She combs her hair with one hand. She still aches in two or three places; there is a bruise on her left arm, her right knee is slightly skinned. It seems to her very strange to be here; she's no longer sure what happened.

On tiptoe she goes to the door of the bathroom. She

studies herself carefully in the mirror; she raises her chin, turns her head, observes closely the little scratch over her cheekbone; she stretches her lips. On a shelf under the mirror there are jars of essences, bottles and phials made of colored glass, labels written and decorated by hand. Lise takes a honey cream and sniffs it; she spreads a little on her forehead and cheeks, with circular movements of her fingertips. The cream has a faint odor of beehive, in tune with the warm light of the lamps. There is a knock at the door.

Lise looks around, panic-stricken. She seizes a blue towel and wraps herself in it; she comes out of the room and looks for her clothes, but can't find them. She goes back into the bathroom, sees a robe hanging from a hook. She comes out again. She opens the door just a crack, holding the towel tight around her.

Outside there is a young maid holding a package. She hands it to Lise and says, "Here. And you can use all the clothes in the closets."

Lise takes the package. She says, "Do you know where Mr. Wesley is? The red-haired man who came here with me?" She speaks distinctly, afraid the girl may not know English except for a small repertory of memorized expressions.

The maid nods, saying, "Third door on your left toward the stairs," rapidly though with a somewhat uncertain accent. She bows briefly and disappears into the corridor.

Lise opens the package, and there are her stockings and pants, her green coverall, washed, ironed, and mended. She throws everything on the bed and goes to open the closet: all sorts of dresses and skirts and blouses and jackets of various colors and fabrics. She runs a hand over them to shift them, and receives rapid tactile impressions, rapid chromatic impressions as the fabrics successively come to the light. She hesitates: she takes out an orange-and-purple dress of soft cotton, holds it to her bosom, checks it in the mirror set inside the door. She slips it on, wriggles to smooth it; she puts her hands on her hips, turns to look at herself in profile. From a hook she removes a belt of blond leather; she fastens it around her waist. She crouches to look at the dozens of shoes arranged side by side in a compartment with a brass pipe running across it. She fishes out a purple pair, with medium heels, and slips them on, forcing her heels into them.

The corridor is silent and well lighted; the walls are white, with two or three pop still-lifes from the sixties. Lise takes a few uncertain steps, not remembering which room is Ted's. She tries to recall the maid's words, but the only thing that comes to her mind is that rapid and uncertain accent, the way the girl moved her lips. She knocks at two doors at random: no answer. She goes toward the stairs, leans on the railing, looks down: two guards in gray-and-red uniform stand motionless on the landing of the second floor. She hesitates on the first step, then goes downstairs.

On the ground floor there are guards in the entrance hall, flanking the doors leading to the corridors. Nobody else can be seen; there are no sounds, no voices. Lise goes past the great glass doors of the entrance, looks at the outside steps, the allée of white gravel, the front garden.

An electric buzzing comes from a corridor. Lise follows it, peers into a room where two maids are running vacuum cleaners along converging lines. She says, "Excuse me, but where can I get some breakfast?" She raises her voice to combat the noise of the vacuuming. The two maids turn and look at her; one of them comes to the door and points out the way.

Lise follows the corridor, enters a little room flooded with light from big windows over the garden: little white tables, white chairs, kumquat trees in pots. Only one of the tables is occupied, by a character in his early forties with a mauve-and-gray-checked jacket, mousy hair, narrow-rimmed glasses. He is reading a book, which he holds open on the cloth, while his left hand stirs a spoon in a bowl.

Lise approaches him with cautious footsteps. She says, "Excuse me, have you by any chance seen a heavyset guy with reddish hair, an American?" She accompanies her words with gestures to indicate Ted's dimensions.

The seated character looks at her hands. He says, "No, I'm very sorry. I don't think so." He has a very English accent, a way of speaking while barely parting his lips. He hesitates between the open book and Lise.

Lise looks around in the empty little room; she pulls out a chair. She says, "Do you mind if I sit here?"

The character says, "No, not at all." He waits politely for a second, then goes back to his reading.

Lise sits down. She clears her throat. She has a faint headache, too. A girl dressed in white comes to her, asks what she would like to have. Lise points to the reader's bowl and says, "The same." The girl slips away. Lise looks around; there are no corners in the room, no sharp meeting of lines at the junction of walls, of window frames, chair backs, table edges. She thinks again of the corridor, of her room, and she can't recall any corners there, either, any angles. The girl in white returns, carrying a tray with a jug of milk, a bowl of cereal flakes, a bowl of hazelnuts, and a little pot of honey.

Lise mixes the flakes and the nuts, pours the milk. The character opposite her goes on reading, intent on his book; he raises his eyes for a moment, to check on her. Lise asks him, "Where has everybody gone?"

It takes him a couple of seconds to focus on the question; he leans back in his chair. He says, "Macno is inaugurating a solar-energy installation somewhere, I don't remember exactly where. Almost everyone went with him."

"Don't you know when they're coming back? When will Macno be back?" Lise asks, looking at his collar.

"I haven't the foggiest notion, to tell the truth," he says.

Lise looks at his hair, which retains a hint of blond under the mouse color; she says, "The fact is, I have to interview him. We're from a television station, me and the cameraman. Macno promised us an exclusive interview."

"Ah, very interesting," the character says, with a glint of doubt in his eyes. He shuts the book.

"Yes," Lise says. She pours a spoonful of honey into the bowl, letting it drip, slow and golden. She says, "We haven't introduced ourselves. My name is Lise Förster." She shifts the spoon to her left hand; she holds out her right.

The character impulsively holds out his left hand, draws

11

it back, extends the right. He says, "How do you do? I'm Henry Dunnell." His movements are awkward, complicated by the length of his arms in his floppy sleeves.

Lise eats a spoonful of muesli, chewing dutifully. Dunnell turns and looks out the window: two guards are passing by on the lawn, in the distance, with two cinnammon-colored dogs on leashes. Lise asks, "What are you doing here?"

"Having breakfast," he says, with an asymmetrical smile.

"I mean here in Macno's residence," Lise says, looking at his uneven teeth, exposed by his smile.

"Oh, botanist, more or less," Dunnell says.

"You're in charge of the garden?" Lise says, pointing to the park.

"That, too," Dunnell says. He turns again to look outside; he says to Lise, "If you like, we can take a little walk."

"Really?" Lise says.

"Of course," Dunnell says. He looks at the table, at his untouched bowl of muesli; he rises, picks up his book.

Lise stuffs a rapid spoonful into her mouth, wipes a drop of milk from her chin. She tries to read the title of Dunnell's book as he makes a futile attempt to slip it into a pocket of his jacket. The title is *Unstable States*. Dunnell intercepts her glance; he smiles slightly. He says, "It's a kind of science-fiction story, but fairly plausible. Or maybe it's really a love story."

They go out through a glass door that opens onto the lawn. Lise narrows her eyes against the light and gazes through her lashes at the gently sloping expanse of grass, the different shades of green in the bushes, the shrubs, the tall trees, the wooded thicket beyond the little lake.

Dunnell leads the way, clumsily, trying to guide her with illustrative gestures. He says, "You must have noticed the difference between the two halves of the park, the front half and this. The palace is also divided in the same way: the front half for official activities, and the rear for all the rest. In any case, *this* is the real park."

They walk on the cropped grass, slowed down by the sun, which glints on Dunnell's eyeglasses and on the water of the distant lake, on the glass of a greenhouse. Dunnell leads Lise along a winding route, brings her close to bushes and trees according to the best angle. He points out plants left and right, isolated or arranged in compositions by shape and color, contrast of leaves, height and thickness. He stops to give Lise time to appreciate a certain view; he studies her reactions.

Lise tries to concentrate: she examines the leaves of a ginkgo, trembling in a light puff of wind; she says, "Very beautiful." Three guards, with walkie-talkies in their hands and submachine guns over their shoulders, pass rapidly at a distance of ten yards; they sketch a salute to Dunnell.

Dunnell points to a reddish bush with an oblique crown. He says, "Look at this *Rhyvia Ponewiczi*. We brought it here from Bolivia because Macno liked its shape. I didn't think it would take, but Macno made it a question of principle, practically. He came here every morning to see. When he was away, he telephoned me to ask how it was getting on."

Lise's fingers brush the reddish leaves; they fall back into place. She says, "Did Macno personally choose the plants in this park?"

"Of course," Dunnell says. "We discussed it, naturally, but he decided almost everything. The only thing he let me do on my own was the façade side, because it had to be formal and academic and it didn't interest him. The only thing he added himself was the little stand of bamboo."

They go into a garden of citrus trees, the foliage carefully tended. Dunnell, with familiar eyes, checks the bitter oranges and the sweet oranges, the mandarins and tangelos, the lemons and grapefruit and clementines, citron, lime, chinotto, bergamot. He says, "Macno believes that citrus plants are extraordinary, much more precious than any others. Every now and then he says that the only positive feature of this capital is that you can grow citrus trees in the ground."

Lise turns to look at the palace. She says, "And Macno knows everything about plants."

"No, but he knows everything he needs to know," Dunnell says. He studies the form of a mandarin branch; he says, "When he decided to transform this place into his official residence, the old park was a total wreck. Macno had some ideas about what to do with it, but they were vague. That's when he got in touch with me."

"He telephoned you?" Lise asks.

"Well, he had an assistant call me," Dunnell says. "Naturally, when I heard her voice on the phone explaining that Macno wanted to consult me, I was bewildered. I thought: This Latin dictator wants to create a bizarre park. You know what Macno's image is abroad. But the minute I got here and met him I realized what an extraordinary person he is. I mean, *anybody* who meets Macno realizes that."

Lise says, "So you planned the park together." She

has a vision of him and Macno in the old, decrepit park: hands on hips, beside the remains of a cedar of Lebanon.

"We argued for weeks," Dunnell says. "Macno always managed to find the time, in spite of all the fundamental things he had to do. Sometimes we would sit up all through the night, debating and looking at videotapes and reading some old manuals he had got hold of, and then at half past five in the morning he would go have a shower and begin his day, traveling from one part of the country to another, meeting people, persuading them, making plans and programs. I used to wonder where he managed to find the energy to concern himself with the trees, too. Now and then I felt almost guilty. But that's how he is: he has this sort of eagerness to discover the mechanism of things, to grasp the keys. And he never divides things into more important and less important. Those nights, three years ago, we talked about grafting and transplanting and pruning, and I realized he had the same tension, the same intensity as when he dealt with affairs of state."

With pensive steps they leave the citrus garden, turn back toward the distant palace. In the lawn there are five or six cubic holes, piles of earth and sacks of peat beside each hole. Dunnell looks at them; he says, "Macno had a lot of other ideas for this park, but lately he hasn't been able to think about it. I don't want to do anything without him, so everything's in abeyance." He takes off his glasses, polishes them with a handkerchief. He says, "The problem is that he can't resign himself to slowness. He can't bear the idea of waiting years for a plant to grow the way he wants. He would like to have it big immediately, and when he sees that's impossible he loses interest. He can't bear dead seasons, enforced delays. I believe they remind him too much of other slow things he has to deal with."

Lise listens to his tone, so meekly admiring, so lacking in conditions or reservations, and she feels growing inside her a strange yearning for everything she doesn't know about Macno and perhaps will never know. As they walk along a verbena border, she asks Dunnell, "Do you know Macno well?"

Dunnell gives her a sidelong glance. He is thin and disheveled, his checked jacket too big for him. He says, "Every now and then I think I do. But I'm never really sure. He has so many layers."

They walk toward the palace, and neither of the two seems interested in the plants any more.

On the lawn outside the glass door Ted is standing, his arms folded. He is wearing an old-fashioned suit, sand-colored, a bit short in the sleeves and trousers, the buttons straining. When they are still four meters off, he says to Lise, "So that's where you were. I looked all over the place for you."

"I looked for you, too," Lise says, coming up to him. "I didn't know which room was yours."

"You could have asked," Ted says. He stretches forward to kiss her on the brow; she turns toward Dunnell; Ted kisses her on the left temple.

Lise waves her hand and says, "Henry Dunnell. Ted, the cameraman."

"Hello," Ted says, his tone suggesting the introduction has slightly offended him.

All three look at one another for a couple of minutes; then Dunnell says, "I'm afraid I must run now. But you'll be staying on in any case, I hope? I imagine it'll take a bit of time for the interview."

"Oh yes, two days at least," Lise says. "See you around."

"Yes," Dunnell says, heading for the glass door.

Ted waits until he has gone inside; he says, "Who was that?"

"A botanist," Lise says. "Very nice. He's been here with Macno from the start. I believe they're close friends."

Ted looks at the silent garden; in a low voice he says, "Apparently they've all gone off to inaugurate some solar-energy installation."

"I know," Lise says, irritated by his investigator tone.

"Too bad. We could have shot something," Ted says. He points to the palace, reflecting the sunlight; he says, "There's a lot of people here usually. I got a maid to explain it all to me. There's Macno's staff. They work in the front part of the building; and there's a lot of guests, who stay in the other half. It seems he invites people from all over the world, and he keeps them here as his guests for months on end, all expenses paid. Musicians— I don't know what—painters, chorus girls. Anybody who occurs to him, I think, and they stay here as his guests. He must be an incredible megalomaniac."

"What do you know about him?" Lise asks quickly. "You don't know him at all."

"And you do, I suppose?" Ted says. "And anyway, why do you have to be so hostile now?" He reaches out and tries to grasp her arm with his hand.

"I'm not hostile," she says, eluding him. She heads for the glass door.

Ted follows her along the corridor; he walks at her side. He says to her, "You're very elegant."

"Thanks," she says. "It was in the closet in my room."

"This was in the closet, too," Ted says, touching his sand-colored jacket. "But it's not such a good fit, is it?" He pats himself on the stomach, trying to make her smile.

Lise makes an effort to keep a straight face; she smiles. She says, "No, it isn't, if I must be frank."

Ted laughs, relieved; he takes her arm. He says, "Don't let's quarrel, Lizzie, please. We're guests here in Macno's palace and he said he would grant us an exclusive interview and we're practically rich and famous, and instead of being all pleased and pleasant, you turn hostile on the slightest pretext."

"I'm only annoyed when you talk in that superficial tone," Lise says, looking into a room full of musical instruments. By one of the big windows a young man with dark glasses and one leg in a cast is striking the keys of a vibraphone with two sticks. He is concentrating so hard, or his eyeglasses are so dark, that he doesn't notice the presence of Ted and Lise, not even when they have come into the room.

"I won't do it again," Ted says. "I promise."

"All right," Lise says. She doesn't draw away when he bends to give her a kiss on the cheek.

T H R E E

Lise looks at the clock and it's ten in the evening. On the video screen Vee Dawny is performing a multiple pirouette to the simple buzz of the audio, turned down to zero.

She goes and washes her face with cool water; she slaps herself a few times on the cheeks, to rid herself of the dullness from daytime sleep. She digs into the closet, takes out two or three dresses; she chooses one of dark-green silk, slips it on. She puts her left hand on her right shoulder; she arches her brows.

There is no one in the corridor, but music rises from

the staircase at the end, and the undefined seething of many voices at once. Lise knocks hard on Ted's door. From inside his voice says, "Be right there." Lise raps again with her knuckles, more quickly.

"Coming. Who is it?" Ted's voice says, already more alarmed. The door opens; Ted sticks his red head out. He says, "Jesus, you nearly gave me a heart attack."

"Don't be so tense," Lise says. "We're guests now."

Ted says, "Come in for a minute, while I finish dressing." He is in shirt sleeves, a pair of blue slacks, shiny black shoes. His room is spacious and well furnished, even though it is less elegant than Lise's. He takes a blue jacket from the wardrobe, slips it on; this one is also short in the sleeves, tight at the waist.

"Don't you have anything that fits you better?" Lise says, walking around him.

"No," Ted says. "I've never had so many suits to pick from in my whole life, and not one that's the right size." All the same he carefully inspects himself in the mirror; he adjusts his collar.

"You're very elegant," Lise says, looking at his ankles, practically bared by the blue slacks.

Ted says, "Cut it out, you little bitch." He pulls down one sleeve of the jacket, tries to cover at least a part of his stiff white cuff; he gives up the idea. He says, "I believe they've all come back. There must be a party going on downstairs."

Both listen; the throb of the electric bass can be felt through the floor.

They go down the stairs, Lise first, unsteady on her too-high heels. The guards on the second-floor landing don't focus their eyes when the two go by, sticking to the banister.

The other guards have white holsters at their belts and dull black walkie-talkies, earpieces in a single ear. They pretend to be completely impermeable to the music and the voices that spill from the wide-open doors of a drawing room and flood the corridors. Lise and Ted cross the entrance hall, peer in at the door.

The music is electronic, compressed, and cadenced. The room is big, full of loud people, vibrating beneath the light of the chandeliers. The bass and the percussion form a rapid texture into which the laughter and cries are interwoven, the emphasized words, the words thrown away, the drawling of vowels, the rolled "r"s, the chirps and whispers, the grumbles, the coughing. And with the voices the movements are interwoven: slow and sudden and repeated in ten different places; the forward bends and the backward, the turning of heads and chests, the diagonal shifts that assemble people in swarms, scatter them into trios and couples and singles, who cross the room looking for new aggregations.

Lise enters cautiously, followed a pace behind by heavy-footed Ted. There are very elegant and formal women, women in filmy fabrics that reveal long thighs and velvet backs; girls in sweat suits, girls with eyeglasses and floppy clothes; very young girls with narrow hips, women with curly gray hair. There are men with broad backs and thick arms, thin men with sharp features; men dressed in Macno's semi-Japanese style, and men in traditional suits like Ted's. There are exotic men and women, with black or red skin, dressed and posed so as to underline their

21

peculiarity and make it seem almost theatrical. All are in full control of their voices and their movements: bent on being themselves and belonging to the party.

Lise makes her way forward, not knowing exactly where to go or where to stop. Ted follows her automatically, touches her elbow to point out someone to her and comment, with glances, on the situation. At a table where great wooden bowls are brimming with hazelnuts and radishes and cubes of cheese and tiny hard-boiled quail eggs, she says to him, "Will you stop staring at everybody like that?"

"Why? Any law against it?" he says, almost on top of her, turning his head in many directions. He picks up a handful of nuts, fills his mouth, chews. He says, "Now that we've managed to get inside here, might as well take a look around. Right?" With little eyes he observes the passage of a girl with a well-shaped behind.

Lise eats a slice of candied mango; teetering on her heels, she takes a few steps. Ted comes after her, breathing down her back, heavy and inelegant; he says, "Look at the way that one's dressed." He tries to claim her attention at every moment, doesn't let her go away, grazes her leg with his leg.

At a certain point Lise says to him, "It may not be necessary for us to be actually *always* on top of each other."

"Now, don't start that again," he says, with a hurt air. But he doesn't follow her when she goes off a few meters, into the thick crowd.

Lise takes a glass of cider from a tray, drinks half of it, looking at the faces and the movements. She leans with one leg against a little sofa where a girl with beehived hair is sitting with a man in a blue jacket edged in red.

The girl is holding a thin-stemmed goblet in her fingers; she looks at it against the light. She says, "I heard they caught two armed characters in the garden yesterday afternoon." "They weren't armed," the man in the blue jacket says, looking away.

Lise follows his movement and realizes that everyone's eyes, gestures and attitudes are converging on one point in the room, where the vibration seems more intense. Nobody has turned in an explicit way; the tension is oblique, barely dissimulated under the surface, under every approach and distancing and turn of trunk and tilt of head. Lise seeks the center of the vibration, and through the filter of people she sees Macno.

He is standing near a lamp with an orange light; he is talking, and those around him sway at every movement of his lips.

Without thinking, Lise goes toward him, picking her way among backs and chests and ankles. It is hot now; the sound of the interwoven voices rises and falls with the rhythm of the music.

When she is four meters from Macno, the bared smiles, the sticky movements of the girls and women near him come into focus: the attempts to catch his eye, to prolong his attention for a tenth of a second. And the men have the same attitude, the same eagerness to linger in his aura.

Lise tries to assume a casual manner; she looks to one side, raises her glass to her lips. But she has to hold out against those who try to glide into her place, jostle her aside with feigned innocence to move closer to Macno.

Macno is speaking, and his every smile spreads out like circles in water, is communicated to those around him and to those behind them and those behind them.

The closest girls and women try to move still closer; they look at him with parted lips, their teeth sparkling; they exploit a movement of his to graze an arm or a hip. He does nothing to gain distance: he bends his head, he turns to the left and to the right.

Lise tries not to veer too much toward him; she remains oblique, magnetized, at a distance of four meters.

He turns at one point and sees her. He smiles at her, makes a little gesture of greeting.

Lise rises on tiptoe, smiles after him, but he is already turning elsewhere, distracted by the scrimmage of voices, gestures, requests for gestures. There is a time gap between the two smiles, but it isn't clear when. Lise remains suspended for a moment, without thoughts, and the men and the eager girls thrust her back with brief movements of hip and thigh that aim at narrowing the circle around Macno.

Lise is ten meters from him, her cheeks burning at the thought of having gone out on a limb so stupidly. All the same, she can't stop looking at him as he moves: the circle of people breaks to allow him to pass, it scatters into single individuals, who form a wake in his footsteps.

Lise drinks more cider; she drinks thick red wine. She observes faces above the rim of the glass, listens to fragments of marginal conversations. Every time she seeks Macno with her eyes, she sees him at a different place in the room, surrounded by different people.

Someone waves a hand before her face; Ted says, "Can you see me, Miss Förster?" His eyes are gleaming; his movements have a childish euphoria. He says, "Can you believe we're really here? I'm still not sure." He turns his

24

head in many directions. He puts his hand on her hip; he says, "It's all your doing."

But his accent now embarrasses her, his excitement: a big baby needing reassurance. She says, "Don't make scenes, please."

"What scenes am I making? Would you mind telling me?" he says with a shade of hurt in his eyes. He takes the glass of red wine from her hand, drinks a long sip. He turns to look.

A few paces away, in the center of a group of people, there is a woman of about twenty-nine, with an elegant figure. She is wearing a green dress similar to Lise's, but with a lower hem, over her knees. Her hair is gathered at her temples with elaborate simplicity, held by two little brooches of gold filigree.

"Melissa. Macno's wife," Ted says in a low voice.

"Don't shout," Lise says, embarrassed. She looks at the woman with a show of nonchalance, thinking that she is just a bit thinner and paler than the way she looks on television. The people around her are eager, but less so than the ones around Macno.

Ted sinks onto a low sofa, motions Lise to sit down beside him. Lise sits down, tries to maintain a few centimeters' distance; she pushes aside Ted's arm as he tries to put it around her waist. They are silent, looking at the people, who talk and gesticulate and approach and go off as the night gradually advances. Every now and then they pick a glass from the tray that a waiter lowers for them; they drink different wines, without much attention.

Ted stands up, says, "I'm going to hunt for the can; God knows where the hell it is. I'll be right back." He goes off, looking around, clumsy in his blue suit with its too-short sleeves and trousers. Lise looks at him with embarrassment and tenderness and irritation, too mingled to isolate one feeling from the other. He turns at about fifteen meters, and signals to her to say again, I'll be right back.

Lise takes some more little sips of wine, her left arm resting on the back of the sofa. The crowd seems to move with greater excitement, laugh more often. The musicians on the little dais at the end of the room drive the beat harder; the music's intensity increases. Lise listens and watches still, with the impression that she is not able to perceive the nuances clearly, that she is seeing everything with a tourist's eyes. She gets up, walks at random, looking at the people more closely. Macno is no longer in the center of any circle, but the tension remains, beneath the gestures and the expressions: everyone continues speaking fast, turning his head. Lise pauses at the edges of the conversations, and a couple of men smile at her, say to her, "How's it going?" They ask her questions about herself and her work; they say to her "interesting" or "sounds wonderful." But they are too anxious and their attention doesn't last long: they nod, and are already looking for other contacts with their eyes.

A girl with a slender neck starts dancing; she moves her arms over her head, shakes her hair. Other women imitate her, then some men. Lise glides toward the great windows looking out on the darkness; she watches the movements and the reflected lights. She walks to a French window, opens it. She goes out.

Outside, the air is warm, barely stirred by a wisp of breeze. Lise sniffs the perfume of eucalyptus and horsemint, the slow perspiration of the garden at night. She crosses the strip of white gravel that separates her from the lawn, the beams of the little spotlights trained on the palace. She walks on the lawn, looks at other luminous swaths that here and there make a tree or a group of shrubs emerge from the darkness. Her slim heels sink in at every step; she slips off her shoes, walks barefoot on the damp, springy grass. There is a sliver of moon in the May sky, veiled by insubstantial clouds. Lise turns, and three meters behind her, his hands in his pockets, his dark eyes shining, there is Macno.

He comes close to her; he says, "Were you bored to death in there?" He waves vaguely toward the palace behind him.

"No," Lise says, breathing slowly.

Macno says, "And they didn't all seem unbearable idiots to you?"

"Who?" Lise says.

"All of them," Macno says. He digs in the grass with the tip of one foot. He says, "God knows what sort of picture you must have of this place. A kind of parking lot for frivolous courtiers."

Lise remains silent. She makes an effort to think of something to say, but the few ideas that whirl in her head are swollen, without corresponding words.

Macno takes a step; Lise follows him, a half-meter to his right. They walk beyond a mimosa tree illuminated by a spotlight. Macno says, "I'm very sorry about yesterday."

"Oh, it doesn't matter," Lise says hurriedly. She tries to put together an attitude, to achieve a minimum of perspective. But the idea of having spoken to him shamelessly the day before seems to her far away, out of focus.

He says, "All these security measures are apparently indispensable, but the fact is that once they're set up they don't discriminate." His voice is warm, though less careful than when he speaks on television: it has more angles, more irregularities of tone.

Lise tries to follow up on his words, add something or oppose them while it's easy; she hesitates, and the subject moves further and further away. In the end she says, "Surely it can't be pleasant to have to be so careful all the time." Her tone and the sentence don't go well, and are late, in any case.

Macno says "What," turns toward her, tries to make her out in the semidarkness.

She stops, and a shaft of light reveals her: blonde and pale and dressed in green. The light shifts to Macno; it is lowered immediately. Two guards salute and slip off into the darkness, behind their flashlight.

"You see?" Macno says. "It's hard to take a step."

They are facing each other under the foliage of a great eucalyptus, whose pale trunk can barely be discerned. Lise thinks how little nocturnal space there is between them; and how much it could still shrink. For an instant she is sure that Macno is thinking the same thing, and immediately afterward she is sure no longer. She would like this suspended state, open to the forces of attraction, to go on forever, and at the same moment it is already finished. Macno turns; Lise turns with him.

Side by side they look at the palace: the great windows that contain lights and sounds and movements like the glass of an aquarium. They are quite close, even if not as before; Lise wonders how irreparable the loss of a moment is. They look at the palace for four or five minutes, without saying a word. Then Macno moves; they retrace their steps.

"What were you thinking?" he asks abruptly, when they are thirty meters from the palace.

"When?" Lise says, gripped by panic.

"Before," he says. "When we were standing still."

Lise hesitates a second; she says, "I was thinking that this side of the palace is never seen on television, and millions of people try always to imagine it on the basis of the façade, each in a different way, but never in the right way." She feels clumsy, false; she gnaws her lip.

"No," Macno says. He looks at the windows, from which music begins to leak: the cymbals and the Charleston of the drums over the notes of the electric bass.

They cross the glow of the spotlights, they pause on the white gravel a few meters from the wall where Palmario is waiting, motionless. Macno turns toward Lise.

They look at each other for two or three seconds, again suspended at a short distance, but in full light. Macno says, "Listen: we must talk soon about the interview."

"All right," Lise says, with a slightly askew smile.

Macno bends, takes her hand, kisses it. The contact lasts a tenth of a second or less: almost simultaneously, he is already three steps away and she is looking at him with surprise.

"I'll see you tomorrow," Macno says at the little door that Palmario is holding open for him. He makes a rapid gesture, disappears inside.

Lise says "Good night," watches the door close. She takes a few steps back toward the lawn, does a euphoric little turn.

FOUR

At the end of the corridor Ottavio Larici is waiting with his arms folded: nervous and elegant, in his semi-Japanese gray jacket, his very short brown hair cropped close at the nape, his blue eyes darting as soon as Macno and Ester and Palmario are near him.

Macno says, "Hey, Ottavio," embraces him. It is an act of warmth, and long practiced; an assertion or a confirmation more than a simple impulse.

"Macno," Ottavio says. His return embrace is only a succession of ritual movements, performed with style. He says, "Everything's ready," opens the door.

Uto, seated in one of the little chairs, hardly turns when he hears them come in; he stands, says "Hello." The buttons of his jacket seem to have been fastened with some difficulty at the level of his stomach; his thick blondish hair looks as if it had been cut with a lawn mower. He pauses longer than necessary in Macno's embrace, pats his back with his stubby hands. He says, "I'm very anxious to see."

"Now you'll see it," Macno says, freeing himself. He goes and sits in the last row of seats, Ester at his side. He looks at the two milky screens at the other side of the little room. He says, "Well?"

"We're ready, we're ready," Ottavio says, at the video projector. He turns out the lights.

On the lefthand screen a crowd appears, waiting: men and women and children assembled, looking up. They are all dressed in full-summer clothes, with short-sleeved T-shirts and canvas hats and sunglasses a month and a half before the right season. On the other screen there is an empty platform, with a microphone in the center, piles of huge loudspeakers at either side.

In the little room Ottavio comes and takes a seat; Uto coughs. Macno slides down against the chair's back, drums two fingers on the back of Ester's hand.

On the left screen the crowd suddenly comes to life. They wave their arms, applaud, shout unintelligible phrases. On the right screen Macno strides across the platform. He is dressed in black in his usual style, with a red band around his brow, his eyes underlined by a touch of black, which makes them more legible at a distance. He stops in the center of the platform, removes the microphone from its pole, takes a half-step backward.

On the left screen the crowd applauds harder: women blow kisses, children are held up in their fathers' arms, girls scream shrilly. On the right screen Macno waits, breathes slowly. Then, with a brusque movement, he holds the microphone to his lips, says, "how are you?" His voice comes from the loudspeakers strong and intense, every nuance sustained. The crowd replies with a shout that spreads and spreads until it loses definition in the recording.

In the little room Macno pushes himself forward and bites his lip. He says, "Jesus."

On the right screen Macno begins to speak. As he speaks, he walks from one end of the platform to the other, his step light. His gestures, his figure, the shadings of his voice are so familiar to the people observing him that they arouse enthusiasm by the mere fact of being there, the mere fact of confirming the details of the television image that has entered so many times the houses of them all. Macno has only to extend his right arm, move it in an arc that takes in the whole audience, say "as all of you well know" in his familiar tone, and he sparks an unthinking explosion of applause that carries away each of the listeners and contracts his features in a spasm. He goes on like this for some minutes: without saying anything special, simply sounding the distance between himself and the crowd, testing reflexes, absorbing reactions. And when the expectation in the faces on the left screen has risen and risen and the eyes are full of anticipation, anxious for new guarantees, Macno drops his platform gestures; his voice loses sharpness, shades into reflecting tones; his sentences extend in parentheses that create a veil of puzzlement around the sentences that preceded them. The people on the left screen look up, silent, uncertain about what they should recognize, what they should respond to, and how. Macno stops, addresses a single group of listeners, a single person. He turns toward the camera, and in the early-afternoon light the sweat can be seen on his brow. The left screen shows single faces as they proceed from attention to puzzlement to a still slower expression. Macno speaks, motionless in the center of the great platform, as if he were talking to himself.

In the little room Macno says, "All right, all right, we get the idea."

Ottavio slips through the darkness to turn off the projector. The screens are milky again; the lights come back on, reveal every corner of the room: the dead white of the walls, the brilliant orange of the seats.

Uto turns, stiff-necked, one arm pressing the back of the seat; he says, "Listen, it's not so bad."

The words remain suspended in the air for a couple of seconds.

Macno says, "Look, Uto, I can put up with a lot, but how can you say a thing like that? Even a child can see it's lousy."

"You're exaggerating," Uto insists. "That's not so. The first part isn't bad at all."

"That's right. It's not bad until I start talking," Macno says.

With nervous hands Ottavio fiddles with the video projector, avoids looking at the others.

"What do you think?" Macno asks him. "It's not so bad?"

Ottavio raises his eyes from the projector; he says, "All right, you can't expect more. They weren't carried away."

33

"Why can't I expect more?" Macno says, leaning on one elbow.

"Because you can't," Ottavio says in a higher voice. "You know that better than I do. If you had given it just a little more power, you'd have carried them away like you wanted."

"But I didn't have the slightest desire to carry them away," Macno says. He sinks again against the back of the chair; he says, "I didn't give a damn about carrying them away. There are a million things in life that interest me more than going out and carrying away crowds."

Ester looks at him, close, alert. Uto looks at him, stopped on the brink of a sentence.

Ottavio says, "All right, okay. We're not here to talk about what interests us most in life. We're only trying to put together a decent video for the Third Anniversary, and so far, with four speeches taped live, we might have at most two minutes of stuff we can use."

"Don't start talking about minutes we can use," Macno says. "I've already told you a dozen times I want a complete speech. I don't have any intention of cheating."

Ottavio lowers his hands; he says, "Macno, I'm only trying to do my job."

"And I'm trying to do mine," Macno says. He looks at the floor, looks at Ester, presses the hand she keeps ready.

Uto gets out of his seat, comes closer. He says, "Macno, the question is that we have less than a month and a half from today to the Third Anniversary. And on the day of the Third Anniversary we *have* to have a speech we can broadcast."

"And we can't broadcast one that doesn't work," Ottavio says, his hand on the projector.

Uto says, "We have to admit that this isn't an easy moment for Macno, and you can't expect—"

"All right, all right," Macno says, standing up. He goes to Ottavio, says, "And what should I do, in your opinion?" He doesn't look him in the face; he looks at the door.

Ottavio says, "Macno, let me at least have a try with the crowd. I'll leave your speech the way it is; I'll just make another edit with the crowd. I won't change a word of what you said." He has a reasonable look in his eyes, a reasonable way of deploying words.

"No," Macno says, still without looking at him. But he doesn't move; he stares at the floor.

"Macno," Ottavio says, trying to catch his eyes. "I'll make a rough cut. You come and see it day after tomorrow, and if you're not persuaded, we'll throw it away. At least we have an option. It doesn't cost us anything."

Macno looks at him just for an instant; he goes toward the door. He says, "If you feel like working for nothing."

"Yes," Ottavio says. "Just to have an option."

"Good-bye," Macno says. He shows Ester out; he leaves, slams the door.

Ottavio looks at Uto: with the eyes of someone who has just made an enormous effort.

FIVE

The little tables in the breakfast room are now all occupied by people eating, alone or in couples or in little groups. There is a girl with a vertical hairdo who handles her silver with stylized movements; a character with the back and arms of a weightlifter, spinning an ear of corn in the butter; a tall, thin black man dressed in a cream-colored suit, who taps his spoon on the rim of a teacup. There is Ted by a window, and Lise comes up behind him, gives him a pat on the shoulder.

He turns, focuses her; he says, "Look who's here." His face is pink, relaxed; a maroon homespun suit in semi-

36

Japanese style makes him seem at once more frivolous and more solid.

Lise sits down; she orders raspberries with lemon juice from the waitress who comes over to her.

Ted pushes aside a crystal bowl with traces of yogurt; he says, "May I ask where you've been all this time? I came and knocked on your door and nobody was there."

"I was asleep," Lise says. "I didn't hear you. I just got up." His possessive attention now irritates her, and also arouses her lightly as it brushes, groping, her encounter with Macno last night.

"What about last night?" Ted says. "Where did you disappear to? I looked for you everywhere."

"I waited at least half an hour for you," Lise says. The waitress arrives with the bowl of raspberries, sets it on the table. Lise says, "You said you'd be right back, and then I didn't see any more of you."

"It took me an hour to find the can," Ted says, one-third reassured. He looks at her white, well-shaped hands as she draws the bowl of raspberries closer. He says, "Wouldn't it all be simpler if we asked them to put us in the same room, really? We're not under any obligation to pretend we're not together."

"We'll talk about it later, Ted, all right?" Lise says. She concentrates on the raspberries.

Ted looks at a girl with hair all in ringlets three tables away: full breasts under a transparent blouse. He shifts his eyes to Lise; he says, "Every now and then I get the impression you're ashamed of me, goddammit."

"That's not true," Lise says, rapidly employing her spoon.

"Then why do you always have this look?" Ted says. "This dumb, embarrassed look?"

"That's not true," Lise says again. "Maybe I'm a bit tense. This isn't the most normal situation in the world, you know."

"But you're fond of me all the same?" Ted asks, his eyes little and keen.

"Of course," Lise says. She hands him the spoon filled with raspberries, says, "Want some?"

"No, thanks," Ted says, three-quarters reassured.

Lise eats the raspberries, inadequate as they are for her late-morning hunger. Between spoonfuls she raises her eyes, looks at the people in the little room: two girls with pointed noses who giggle to themselves, a very pale character with a high forehead, an elegant and silent couple with gray hair, the girl with the slender neck who started the dancing the previous evening. Each person or little nucleus of persons seems to have nothing in common with the others, beyond their presence in the same place: like participants in a cruise with only the cruise in common.

Ted takes a sip of tea; he says, "I ran into Macno in the corridor."

"When?" Lise says.

"While I was on my way here," Ted says. "He was with his usual bodyguard, that animal, and a certain Ester, his private secretary, fairly pretty."

"What did he say to you?" Lise asks, putting her spoon in the empty bowl.

"Nothing in particular," Ted says. "He asked me how things are going, how you are, if we need anything, et cetera."

"He asked how I am?" Lise says, trying to replace Ted's neutral words with images.

"Yes," Ted says. "Oh, he also said we're invited to a Rainer Blume concert in the garden tomorrow night. He didn't make the slightest reference to the interview. Maybe he was waiting for me to ask him something, but the right words didn't occur to me, I don't know." He looks at his left wrist, pinches his watchband. He says, "The fact is, you don't really know how to act with him, because he's so polite and *accessible;* he's not what you imagine when they say dictator. Still, at the same time you sense something under the surface, and, naturally, he *is* a dictator, and you don't know how far you can go before upsetting him and making him decide to have you shot or something." He looks at Lise, who turns her eyes away. He says, "Anyhow, I wasn't able to ask him about the interview."

Lise looks to one side: a curly-headed boy with a Greek profile is saying something into the ear of a woman with violet-tinted eyeglasses.

Ted says, "Maybe it would be better for you to talk to him about it."

"Why?" Lise says without turning.

"Mm, because he certainly pays more attention to you," Ted says. "I'm only the cameraman; you're the interviewer. And, besides, you certainly appeal to him more than I do. Latins are crazy for blonde women."

"Have you finished talking nonsense?" Lise says, her cheeks flushing slightly. She pushes back her chair, says, "Let's go somewhere. I'm fed up with sitting around."

Ted follows her out of the room, while the others at the tables look at them.

"Where do you want to go?" he asks her, trying to keep up with her along the corridor, where other guests are walking arm in arm and chatting in various languages.

"Oh, just to take a look around," Lise says. Two dark-skinned girls and a blond character of about twenty walk past them, chuckling.

"Let's go this way, then," Ted says; he points to a secondary branch of the corridor that stretches off on the right, down a few steps. He says, "I took a couple of turns yesterday and this morning, and I've just about got it all figured out."

The corridor, in reality, is a gallery with a glass ceiling, over which a climbing plant grows, to ward off the rays of the sun. Lise and Ted look at the potted papyrus plants, the great brilliant-colored canvases on the walls.

Ted says, "In this wing there are a lot of studios for artists, and stuff like that. In the basement there's the gym and the indoor pool and the sauna and all the rest. On the other side there are projection rooms and electronic studios and music rooms; on the third floor, where we are, there are guest bedrooms; and there are dining rooms and rooms for parties, et cetera." He points to right and left, above and below, like a curt guide, inadequately briefed.

Lise goes to a window, looks outside: a tender green lawn, colored by pink anemones and campanulas and California poppies.

Ted says, "That's a kind of patio, but I haven't worked out where the entrance is." He points in the opposite direction and says, in a lower voice, "On the façade side there is the whole official part of the palace. There must be electronic centers and meeting rooms and moviolas and all that. I tried to take a look this morning early, but they sent me back. Polite but firm. You need a pass or something."

"Trying to get yourself arrested for espionage, are you?" Lise says.

They go past a large, luminous room where a sculptor is working, giving quick blows of the scalpel to a block of marble, its shape still vague. They stand there a couple of minutes watching him, until he turns, faintly annoyed. They continue along the corridor.

Ted says, "You realize what it must cost to keep all these people?"

Lise doesn't answer; in a little room she looks at a character with long sparse hair, turning the dials of a video-recording machine, sending forward and backward a tape of Bo Wippett: the little black boy in the silver jacket balancing on the wing of a plane sings, over and over, the refrain of "Baby Be Nice."

"You realize?" Ted says. "Hundreds of people, feeding them, providing drink, amusing them all the time? And anything they ask for, it's given to them. It must cost a *fortune*, by God."

"How can you think only about these things?" Lise says absently.

They turn left in the glass gallery, which makes a U-curve and heads back for the main corridor. Ted tests a door handle; he opens it onto the outside. He says, "This is how you go out into the patio."

They go out into the patio, walk on the grass. There is a little stone fountain spurting water in the center of a double circle of verbena and red geraniums. A flutist sitting on the lawn plays a strange version of "Baby Be Nice": spiral after spiral, further all the time from the original tune. Ted and Lise look at the African daisies, the minuscule blue lupins, the white salvia, the arches of the portico that frames the patio.

Seated on the low wall of the portico, her head resting against a column, is the woman with violet-tinted glasses who had breakfast in the little room. She looks around, pensive; from time to time she holds a small tape recorder to her lips, says something for the tape.

Ted and Lise pass in front of her, give her a wave of greeting.

She says "Hi." She turns off the tape recorder; she says, "You're the Germans from the TV." She has an American accent, very white teeth and thin lips, a determined jaw.

"*She's* German," Ted says, pointing at Lise. "I come from New York."

"What network?" the American woman asks quickly.

"We're free-lance," Lise says.

The American woman looks at her, raises one hand to her forehead to ward off the sun. She is perhaps thirty-five; her bosom is ample, her waist is thin; she is sunburned. She gets up, holds out her hand to Ted, says, "Gloria Hedges. How's everything?"

"Ted Wesley," Ted says. He holds on to her hand; he says, "You mean *the* Gloria Hedges? The Gloria Hedges of *Why Give Up?*"

"Right," Gloria Hedges says with a little smile. She gives her hand to Lise. She says, "I heard about your adventurous arrival, if I may call it that. You two certainly aren't the kind to surrender at the first obstacle, are you?"

"Well," Ted says, "you have to give it a try every now and then."

Gloria Hedges says, "I wanted to come over and meet you last night at the party, but I couldn't get away. In any case I knew we would meet today or tomorrow."

All three look at one another for a few seconds, suddenly having nothing to say. The refrain of "Baby Be Nice" played by the flutist has turned into a Bach fugue that reverberates against the walls of the portico. Some goldfinches whir in the sunshine, come to drink at the rim of the fountain.

Gloria Hedges looks at the California poppies, says, "Fantastic, these gardens, aren't they? A kind of stereotyped English gardener looks after them; his name's Dunnell."

"I know him," Lise says.

"Ah, he's a charming man," Gloria Hedges says. She swings her little recorder by its strap. "How are you getting along here? Have you already settled down, in this rather mad atmosphere?"

"Yes," Lise says, irked by her condescending tone. "What about you?"

"I *belong* to the place by now," Gloria Hedges says.

"Are you writing something?" Ted asks her.

"*Something?*" Gloria Hedges says. "I'm writing a book on *Macno*, naturally. It's a job without any end, because he's such a mine of material. You keep on discovering more and more fascinating things, and after months of work you seem to know less about him than when you began. Eventually it'll turn out to be more like a novel, I really think."

Lise tries not to seem too alert or interested; she glances sideways from time to time.

"What about you?" Gloria Hedges says, addressing Ted as if he were a little boy. "Do you already have an idea for the interview? Have you talked about it with Macno?"

"Yes," Ted says. "I mean, we talked about it with him when we arrived, but not in any great detail. We're going to talk about it, I think, today or tomorrow, as soon as we see him."

Lise narrows her eyes against the sun; she says, "In any case, he's already told us he agrees to it."

"Well, I'm very pleased for you," Gloria Hedges says with a smile all on the surface. "It's a real coup, all right: to arrive like that and *wham*. I don't know if you two realize, but it isn't as if an opportunity like that has been given to many. There are first-rate people who have been waiting for years. I imagine Macno actually liked the idea of taking two young unknowns and putting them ahead of everybody. He always has this wonderful ability to surprise."

Lise and Ted are silent; Lise looks to one side. The flutist stops playing, lies down on his back to take the sun.

"And furthermore, if he said yes to you, that means you have potential," Gloria Hedges says. "Macno has an almost parapsychological way of understanding what's behind people's façades. You'll do a magnificent interview, I'm sure."

"Let's hope so," Ted says.

"We're not interested in an official interview," Lise says. "We want to do a kind of informal chat, mostly. Let Macno talk about *himself*, mostly." It irritates her to stand there justifying and explaining her intentions now; she says, "Something very informal, with no pretense of reconstructing his life and the history of this country and all that." She looks at Ted, who looks back at her, awed and puzzled.

"Well, it seems like a good idea," Gloria Hedges says. "If Macno agrees, it's an excellent idea."

"Macno agrees," Lise says again.

"I'm sure he does," Gloria Hedges says.

Ted says, "Well, we'll be running along. See you around."

"Yes," Gloria Hedges says. "If you need any information, let me know."

"Thanks a lot," Lise says, going toward the door.

"Not very nice, is she?" Ted says when they are in the main corridor.

"She's a *hyena*," Lise says. "Nice, indeed. The *tone* she took—my God!—as if we were two lousy kids who didn't even realize where we are."

"And her books are disgusting, I believe," Ted says. "My sister threw *Why Give Up?* away after she'd read ten pages."

Lise imitates Gloria Hedges' expression; she says, "I'm very pleased for you, my dears."

Ted laughs, says, "What a *slut*."

"Hyena," Lise says again.

"We'll show her the kind of interview we can do," Ted says.

"Yes," Lise says.

They laugh; they cross the entrance hall, where many guests meet, speaking in loud voices.

S I X

The great white tent is illuminated by banks of spotlights that make it shine in the darkness. Other, moving
spots throw shafts of light across the garden: stripes of
brilliant green where they strike the grass or the weft of
a tree's leaves, stripes of milky dust when they are trained
at the sky. The music spreads through the air, only slightly
muted by the canvas.

Inside, on a round platform in the center of a cone of
light, Rainer Blume is producing rapid notes from a series of keyboards arranged on two or three levels around
him. The notes run simultaneously, blurred and coun-

terpoised, from the deep bass to the most crystalline high note, over a ground of electronic percussions that proceed on their own. The beat is hammering and synthetic, a succession of waves of impact compressed into scant space. Rainer Blume runs his fingers over the keys, stretches his thin arms from one instrument to another, grazes buttons and slides levers, presses pedals. His movements precede or follow the notes by a fraction of a second: prolonging, interrupting, shifting keys, doubling the tempos, suddenly switching. The pallor of his face and the whiteness of the light and the electronic quality of the music make his bravura so abstract and remote that they erase the wonder it would otherwise provoke.

Lise and Ted slip through the semidarkness among the people, seated and sprawled and lying down on the cushions; they find a free corner near the fabric of the big tent; they sit down. Ted rolls onto one side, watches Rainer Blume move from one keyboard to another, rapid and obsessed. Lise looks around: the intent spectators, the girls with their legs crossed, the men with glasses in their hands, a couple kissing, a couple giggling, a woman slumped, asleep. A character with a crewcut on her left, looking at her. Lise turns her eyes away.

The character stretches toward her, says, "Excuse me, but I've figured out who you are."

"You have?" Lise says, trying to maintain a few centimeters' distance.

"Of course," the character says, raising his already shrill voice to force it through the tangle of electronic sounds. He says, "I must congratulate you on the audacity you showed."

"Mm," Lise says. She turns toward Ted, but Ted is too caught up by Blume.

The crewcut character stretches again, with his little hand extended; he says, "I'm Uto Rumi." He waits, porcupinelike.

Lise smiles, embarrassed, looks at his contracted little features, his sharp and glistening eyes.

Uto Rumi shifts his cushion nearer, settling in. He says, "I know Macno promised to give you an interview." He chirps almost in her ear, competing with the more and more thudding music; he says, "I imagine you must be pleased."

"Oh yes," Lise says, hoping the volume will continue to rise until it has made ridiculous any effort to talk inside the tent.

But the music, on the contrary, suddenly drops, is reduced to a repetition of low notes on a flat percussion. Uto Rumi says, "I can imagine. It's a wonderful opportunity, isn't it? Besides, you're so young that, if I may speak frankly, I imagine you don't have a long career behind you, and that makes the opportunity all the more extraordinary and lucky, even though when Macno decided to have faith in you it was unquestionably only because he had the certainty that you deserved it, independently of your professional experience, and Macno has an amazing capacity for understanding people at first glance, a word or an expression is enough for him, surely he sensed remarkable qualities in you. . . ." Word by word he enters into considerations that lead to others that lead to others, in the same squeaking tone in competition with the music, which has begun to swell again. He breaks off for a few seconds when the electronic sounds cut in on the same frequency as his voice; he fills these little pauses with a reassuring sign of his hand, to assure himself of her attention and establish a bridge between the last word and the first one after the interruption.

Lise tries to close the contact, to dispel any interest from her gaze; she turns her head toward the stage. But Uto Rumi leaves her no avenue of escape; he starts stretching toward her again, wrapping new tapes of words around her. He says, "It's a shame the two of you got here when the concert was half over, because even though my real musical passion is for the classics, I have to admit that in the face of a talent like this it becomes hard to maintain a distance. . . ."

"Well, Uto?" a voice behind them says. Uto Rumi turns, Ted turns, Lise turns and sees Macno bending forward in the shadows. Her heart flares.

Macno sinks to his knees, says to her, "Isn't Uto driving you crazy? You must have realized he can go on talking to infinity if he isn't stopped." He speaks without shouting, and yet his voice is distinct above the music.

From behind, a girl with thick hair shoves a cushion at him; he sits down, gathers in his legs. Ted smiles at him, clumsy and anxious. Uto Rumi smiles. Lise breathes slowly.

Macno gives Uto Rumi a little tap on the shoulder; he says to Lise, "You know that once, when there was a Parliament, Uto talked for six hours without interruption? Honestly."

Uto Rumi snickers, pleased that Macno is talking about him; he half-closes his eyes. Lise tries to maintain a graceful position: twisted on one hip, balanced between Macno and the concert.

With his head Macno points at the cone of light where Rainer Blume is frantically moving his hands: the fingers multiplied on the keyboards to produce a succession of circular frequencies. He says, "What do you think of him?"

"He's fantastic," Ted cries, bending to one side. "He's the best. I have all his videos at home."

"I don't know," Lise says, trying to cut Ted out of her field of vision. "He's a bit too cold, perhaps. A bit too technological. He doesn't drive me crazy."

"No," Macno says. His eyes are alert, as if her opinion interested him very much. He says, "That's true. He doesn't do anything for me, either. He's stolid." Now he has to raise his voice, because the intensity of the music continues to increase. He shouts, "And I don't give a damn about electronic percussion and synthesizers. I like *real drums, electric guitars.* I like music you can dance to and remember and hum in the street!"

Uto Rumi tries to protest or add something, but his voice is hopeless against the electronic vibration that climbs and climbs: he moves his lips but not a word is audible. Macno turns toward the girl with the thick hair, who leans forward to say something in his ear.

Lise goes back to watching the stage; she is crooked and taut, ready to turn at the first word from Macno. She looks at the musician in the cone of light, and her attention is all behind her. She inhales the subtly musky perfume of Macno, his presence so near. The scene in the center of the tent seems poorly defined to her; she feels herself distilled inside a languor that grows more intense every second at the thought of how precarious this nearness is.

The music continues to rise upward, the notes ascend in dizzying spirals; the beat becomes more and more excited, closer and closer, until it skips the spaces between the bars and melts into the frequencies that are spun out higher and higher, in a single oscillation almost painful to the eardrums. Everyone listens, carried away, ensnared, and suddenly the music is over; Rainer Blume is standing on the little circular stage and makes his way among the keyboards, comes almost to the edge, bows. The crowd stands up, applauds frantically.

Macno stands up; Uto Rumi, Lise, Ted, the girl with thick hair behind him get up. The applause grows; Rainer Blume bows. The lights come on: the big tent is bright, the applauding people regain substance and color. And in a second they have all turned around, they are applauding in the direction of Macno. There are whistles of enthusiasm, cries, smiles multiplied and remultiplied. Macno bows his head slightly, takes a step to one side. Uto Rumi claps his little spatula-hands hard, says "Bravo!" Ted applauds, smiles with his whole mouth. Lise hesitates, brings the palms of her hands into contact a couple of times. Macno makes a generic sign of gratitude; he repeats it. In a low voice he says, "That's enough, enough. Let's get out of here."

They are at the edge of the tent and Palmario opens a path, undoes a hook, and lets Macno slip out. Uto Rumi, the girl with thick hair, Lise slip out after him. Ted remains caught in the crowd that presses to follow them; Palmario closes the tent again.

They walk on the damp grass as the rumble of applause is still coming from the tent, the hundreds of excited voices. Lise is beside Macno. She is afraid of seeing him run off immediately; she says to him, "They certainly are enthusiastic."

He says, "They are?" He looks at her just for a moment; he moves his eyes toward the dark part of the garden.

Uto Rumi says, "The extraordinary thing is to see the confirmation, every time the occasion arises, of how Macno—"

"Lise," Macno says, turning to her. "About the interview you want to make. We must talk about it."

"Yes," Lise says, caught off guard. "Whenever you want. When you have time. There's no hurry."

"Of course there's a hurry," Macno says. He turns to look at the white tent, the people who are beginning to pour out of it.

Uto Rumi and the girl have stopped a couple of meters away, in the attitude of people who don't want to eavesdrop on a private conversation. Two men who look like bodyguards stand a few paces from Rumi; Palmario is surveying the scene generally.

Macno says, "Maybe we can see each other tomorrow."

"All right," Lise says.

"I'll let you know one way or another," Macno says. "Then we'll talk a bit."

Lise remains a few centimeters from him, unsteady on her heels. She tries to think of something to add, and meanwhile the people pouring from the tent come toward them, heading for Macno with eager smiles. And when a phrase comes to her lips, he is already overwhelmed by the first people, shouting and gesticulating on the lawn illuminated by the spotlights that bring out all the yellow in the pale green.

SEVEN

At seven-thirty in the morning Ted knocks at Lise's door, says, "It's me." Naked and sleepy, she jumps out of bed, snatches a white jersey from a chair, pulls it on, goes and opens the door.

Ted is prancing in the corridor, dressed for jogging: heavy gray pants pulled over his muscular calves. He comes inside, looks at Lise's bare thighs as she pulls the jersey down with one hand. He says, "I knew you were still in bed, dammit."

"I'm ready," Lise says, collecting shorts and socks and jogging shoes.

"Get a move on," Ted says, turning to look at her behind.

"I'm ready," she says from beyond the bathroom door.

Going down the stairs, where the guards are motionless, they step out into the garden. They run on the early-morning grass toward the sun, which has just begun to warm up.

Ted says, "I called New York last night, and Phil won't believe it. He says the interview naturally would be worth a pile of money and it could be sold right away all over the world, no problem; but he doesn't want to hear another word about it until we have it on tape."

"Well, really, Macno said he wants to do it," Lise says, only slightly breathless. "He said it. It's not some vague notion." She runs lightly.

Ted looks ahead, moves legs and arms powerfully. He says, "I know, but Phil says it's happened other times—the character says yes, and then changes his mind at the last moment. He says Walter Wells last year was in this city here for almost a month, and every day they postponed it, until finally he got fed up and went home. It seems this character invited him here a couple of times to lunch and dinner, without even mentioning the interview. And that was Wells of CBS. So you can imagine, with us."

"But this time it's different," Lise says. "Last night, again, he was the one who mentioned it; I didn't ask him anything. He was the one who said we have to talk about it today." Her heart begins to pound from the running; she breathes more deeply.

"I wonder why it should be any different," Ted says. "I mean, a pair of complete unknowns who arrive the way we did: it's a miracle in itself that he didn't slam us in jail. I mean, it's been *two years* since the character gave a real interview, besides the stuff that his press office hands out."

"Would you please stop calling him 'the character'?" Lise says. "At least as long as we're his guests."

"Oh, terribly sorry," Ted says.

They run along the edge of the lake, where wild ducks and geese are swimming: side by side, not looking at each other, intent in different ways on maintaining the same pace.

Ted says, "And when will we be able to film, in your opinion? Realistically speaking." He stamps his feet like a horse as they go past a little uneven patch near a weeping willow.

"Oh, soon," Lise says. "Macno said he wants to do it soon."

They cross a stand of red maples, they enter the thick wood that extends between the lake and the outside wall. They run on the packed earth of a little path, breathe in the shade's dampness. Ted says, "And what does he mean by soon?"

"How should I know?" Lise says. She tries to concentrate on the pace.

Ted clears his throat; he inhales and blows out air from his filled lungs. He says, "Anyway, until I have the tape in my suitcase, I don't believe it, either."

They come out from under the trees, they run in the already stronger sun. In distant parts of the park other guests of the palace are beginning to run or do exercises. Two pairs of guards with dogs on leashes pass each other near the outer wall; they exchange signals.

Ted says, "Do you really want to do this interview, or don't you?"

"Of course I do," Lise says. She is panting more; the sun is burning off the last of the night's dampness. She says, "What kind of dumb question is that?"

"It's just that every now and then you have this kind of absent manner," Ted says. "As if you were thinking of something entirely different."

"Oh, stop it," Lise says. She runs and her heart is beating fast, her forehead is damp with sweat.

They do three more turns around the park. For the fourth time they pass beyond the citrus garden; they stop running. They walk, gasping, swinging their arms. Ted does some knee bends, some push-ups. Lise catches her breath, her hands on her hips; she looks around.

They go back inside the palace, which has already begun to come to life. There are people in the entrance hall and the corridors, people slipping into the little breakfast rooms or coming to peer out into the garden.

At the foot of the stairs an elegant figure with blue eyes stops them; he says, "What a coincidence. I was thinking of you at this very instant." He has an almost perfect British accent, marred only by the heavy "s" in "was" and by the exaggerated clarity of the other words. But his smile is confident, as is the light in his eyes.

Ted looks at him, amazed; Lise, anxious.

The character says, "Ah, forgive me. My name is Ottavio Larici." He kisses Lise's hand, shakes Ted's. He says, "I deal with communications here."

"Yes," Ted says. "I mean, I know that." He smiles, runs the back of his hand over his brow. His breathing still hasn't got back to normal after the running.

Ottavio Larici says, "I wanted to give you some good news. The interview is set for tomorrow, between four and five. You have a full hour at your disposal."

"Fantastic!" Ted says, in his gray sweatshirt with haloes of sweat at the armpits and on the back.

"Fantastic," Lise says.

"I'm very pleased for you," Ottavio says. His features are regular, nicely enhanced by the short haircut, the dark and soft fabric of his suit. He must be about thirty-eight, his eyes barely marked by faint lines of tension and fatigue. He seems in perfect control of the situation and the place, the conversation at the foot of the stairs. He says, "Macno always has terribly little time, and I believe you can imagine what an hour means for him. But he is particularly interested in this interview."

"From four to five, then," Lise says, trying to assume a detached, professional tone despite the jogging clothes and the sweat and the shortness of breath.

"From four to five," Ottavio says. "In Macno's little private study, on the second floor, the other side." He waves in the direction of the study. He says, "Tomorrow morning you'll be given passes, naturally."

"Fine," Lise says, looking at his thin lips.

"Fine," he says with a little concluding nod. Behind him is a girl with high cheekbones, in the attitude of an assistant or a personal secretary; she touches his arm, bends forward to say something to him. "Ah, of course," Ottavio says, turning to Ted. "You may pick up a camera at the video department whenever you like. Just tell them your name."

"Thank you very much," Ted says.

Ottavio kisses Lise's hand, shakes Ted's. He says, "All

the best wishes, then, for your work. We'll meet again before you leave, I hope." He goes off rapidly along the corridor: drawn by thousands of other problems and responsibilities, new sources of tension and of faint lines under the eyes.

"Fantastic!" Ted says, prodding Lise in the ribs as they climb the stairs. Some guests are coming down, chatting, with no purpose beyond having breakfast. Ted says, "It's on, dammit; it still doesn't seem real. I'll call Phil to get the checks ready. You realize what it means?"

"Yes," Lise says, without looking at him very much.

Ted takes her by the arm, says to her, "Do you realize or don't you?"

"Yes, yes," Lise says, thinking of the private appointment with Macno that has vanished forever; of Macno's words last night, now going further and further away.

"You don't seem enthusiastic," Ted says, giving her a long, close look as they walk down the corridor.

"Oh, don't start that again," Lise says. "What am I supposed to do? Jump in the air for joy?"

"Yes, you should," Ted says. "We're rich and famous. Jesus Christ."

E I G H T

At ten minutes to four a guard takes a look at the plastic-sheathed tags that Ted and Lise show him; he opens the door of Macno's little private study; he closes it behind them.

Ted and Lise look around in the empty room. Ted sets the bag with the videotape recorder on the floor. He takes out the camera, weighs it in his hands. He says, "It's unbelievable how little it is, and how light. I didn't think they were out already."

Lise sniffs the air, looks at the few pieces of furniture, without sharp edges. There is a fir desk, and on the desk a gray stone, two marking pens in a red cardboard cup, an old dictionary of synonyms. On the wall opposite there is a video screen; three rows of video cassettes on a wooden bookshelf. On a panel there is the oleograph of an Egyptian statue: pinned up with a thumbtack, in the most casual and temporary way. Actually, the whole room shows few signs of being lived in, bare and luminous as it is.

Ted connects the camera to the recorder, presses two or three buttons. He hoists the camera to his shoulder, aims it at Lise; he says to her, "Do something."

Lise covers her face with one hand, says "Cut it out."

"But I have to test it," Ted says. "We can't run any risks."

Lise lowers her hand, looks at the lens; she sticks out her tongue.

Ted says, "Go toward the window a moment."

Lise goes toward the window, looks outside: the little bamboo grove at the end of the lawn. She offers Ted her profile for about ten seconds, then turns. Her palms are sweating.

"All right," Ted says. He lowers the camera; he studies the angle between the recorder and the screen in the corner.

Lise takes a few nervous steps, looks again at the desk. She sits in a little chair, glances at the pad where the questions to be asked Macno are written in a slanting hand. She rereads the first three or four, and they seem stupid to her and useless, with no indication of a point of view. She tries to think of others, but the only ones that come to her are even more irritating. She stands up, walks with the pad in her hand; she tries replacing the first question with the third, the second with the fourth. She goes and looks at the video cassettes on the shelves, she stretches to read the spines: *The Hybridization of Roses, The Evolution of Gestures, Rolling Stones: European Tour '87, The Tuamotu Islands, The Great Gatsby*. She turns toward Ted, says to him: "Would you do these shelves for me, please?"

Ted says, "Just one minute, sorry." He presses a button: on the screen Lise appears, covering her face with her hand, lowering her hand, looking into the camera, sticking out her tongue.

The door opens. Ted dives to turn off the machine. Lise wheels around.

But it isn't Macno: it's Ottavio Larici. He points to the screen that has just gone blank and says with a little smile, "Definition not bad, is it?"

Ted and Lise look at each other, with reciprocal reproach in their eyes.

Ottavio drops the little smile, says, "Macno asks you please to forgive him; he's terribly sorry but he has to remain in the city because of some serious matters and won't be able to come for the interview. He told me to tell you that he'll try to set it up within the next few days, as soon as possible."

Lise feels her anxiety turn into disappointment; she says "Ah."

Ted looks at the floor, scratches his head.

Ottavio looks at the pad with notes in Lise's hand; he says, "I'm very sorry. The fact is, Macno's always so involved in so many things; I think you realize that. In any case, it's only a question of a few days' postponement."

Lise says, "Of course." She looks at the door, looks at Ted.

63

Ottavio says, "I have a half-hour free now. I don't know—if you feel like asking me some questions for your report, I'm at your disposal." He puts his hands in the pockets of his well-tailored jacket, assumes a pose of being at their disposal.

Lise says, "Thanks, but we weren't thinking of doing anything official. Mostly we wanted to have Macno talk about himself. We had in mind a sort of informal chat rather than an interview."

"Naturally," Ottavio says. "I only mentioned it in case you were interested in having another face on the tape, while you're at it."

Ted looks at Lise, nods his head yes.

Lise looks at Ottavio with puzzled eyes; she says, "But I haven't prepared anything. We'll have to improvise."

"Oh, improvising is no problem for me," Ottavio says. "I don't like interviews myself that are too prepared."

"Fine," Ted says; he crouches to rewind the tape.

"Well, thanks, then," Lise says, still hesitating. She puts down the pad, looks at Ted, awaiting technical instructions.

Ted puts the camera on his shoulder, looks for the best angle. He waves his left hand at Lise, says to her, "By the window. A bit closer."

Lise draws Ottavio toward the window, barely grazing his jacket, which smells of bergamot. He follows her dutifully, tries to foresee her instructions. He says to her, "Am I all right here?"

"Is here all right?" Lise asks Ted.

"Uh-uh," Ted says, his eye in the finder. "Just a shade to the left. There."

Lise rapidly runs a hand through her hair; she asks Ted, "Ready?"

"Rolling," Ted says.

Lise looks into the camera: blonde and nervous in her short, slate-colored dress. She says, "I'm here with Ottavio Larici, the man who—"

"Hold it," Ted says. "Sorry, you're covering him like that."

Ottavio says to her, "I think you should be just a bit farther away."

Lise moves, her fragile professional nonchalance already breaking down. She takes a deep breath, waits for Ted to start over.

"Rolling," Ted says.

Lise says, "Ottavio Larici, in charge of communications. When did you meet Macno?"

Ottavio looks at her, surprised to see her move off camera. He recovers himself at once: slips one hand in his pocket, bends his head slightly. He says, "Five years ago, in the studios of Channel Eight. I'd been working there a short time, and Macno, of course, was preparing *Collisions*."

"And what was Macno like then?" Lise asks quickly.

"Well, a bit younger, naturally," Ottavio says with a smile for the camera. "Five years ago he was twenty-eight. But he wasn't very different from the man we all know today."

"Yes, but apart from the physical aspect," Lise says, "as a person."

"Precisely. As a person," Ottavio says. "He already had that extraordinary magnetism, that extraordinary power of communication. It was obvious he would go a long way. I mean, he was destined to go further, to do much more. You only had to speak with him, or look at him, to realize that."

"And you became friends immediately, when you met?" Lise asks.

"Well, yes. We got along well together immediately," Ottavio says. "At the beginning I was, naturally, intimidated, because Macno was already fairly famous and I was only a kid just back from the States with a degree in mass communications, and I certainly couldn't hope to deal with him as an equal. But as soon as we got to know each other a little bit he was very cordial and straightforward; he spoke with me and asked my opinion without giving himself any airs. Yes, we were on excellent terms immediately."

"How was the idea of *Collisions* born?" Lise asks him.

"The idea in itself wasn't completely new," Ottavio says. His voice doesn't have much body, but the television tone is perfect: balanced between naturalness and professional precision, in harmony with expressions and gestures. He says, "There had already been a couple of programs based on a similar formula, the idea of an interview that didn't kowtow to ministers and political bigshots. What was really new was having someone like Macno to host it. Until then the typical host of that sort of program was one of those middle-aged television figures, bald, with a paunch and a heavy accent, sweaty. They had this slimy way of asking a question, venturing something and then retreating at once, filling in with little jokes, fawning on the interviewer and the camera. It was obvious that they would never put anybody in an awkward position and would stick to questions already agreed on. No viewer could believe they really meant what they were doing, that they would really dig into a subject."

"Whereas Macno . . . ?" Lise asks.

"Macno wanted to dig," Ottavio says. "He didn't want limitations. He wanted to work live, without pre-established subjects or prepared questions or anything. Which made a big difference, compared with other programs of the sort."

"But what gave him the idea of being an anchorman?" Lise asks him.

"He didn't have the idea," Ottavio said. "It was proposed to him. There was this very confused situation, with private TV stations springing up like mushrooms, after decades of the government network's monopoly. It was as if the principle of free competition had just been discovered, and all the networks tried to invent something to beat the others' ratings. The president of Channel Eight was a man named Mino Zefiri, fairly young and very ambitious, and he knew he would have to find something different if he wanted to enlarge his audience in a short time. So he came up with this idea. I remember, he came up with this idea during a meeting at the end of the year. He said that programs with interviews of politicians always work, but we should have someone very different as anchorman—we couldn't keep on with the same old hacks. Then there was a discussion, and somebody asked him who he was thinking about as being different, and Zefiri said, 'I don't know, it ought to be somebody young with charisma, somebody who's popularity is still intact, somebody like Macno, for example.'

That's how the idea was born, even though nobody thought Macno would accept. But somebody who knew him went and proposed it to him, and, unexpectedly, he said yes."

"Why?" Lise says. "Why did something of the sort interest him?"

"Macno's always been like that," Ottavio says. "He's always had this ability to choose new directions, even though it stuns all the people around him. And the ability to understand what are the real questions, where people's real interests are directed. He was doing very well in his career as a singer and actor, he had a great influence on the young—and by then also on audiences of other ages, and he knew that sooner or later he would have to move on, he knew that he would have to turn to more serious things."

"But why interviews with politicians?" Lise asks him.

"Because the politicians were everywhere in this country," Ottavio says with a thin smile. "Once Macno said that the only true pop stars in this country were the politicians. It sounded like a wisecrack, but it was the absolute truth. They were bigger stars than any singer or actor, or athlete, or anyone. They had so taken over the media. The pages of the newspapers, magazine covers, television programs were filled with them. To be sure, nobody loved them or admired them, but they made news. They *were* the news, in this country. The more this country fell to pieces, the more curious people were to see and hear those who had brought it to that condition."

"In what sense exactly was it falling to pieces?" Lise asks.

Ottavio folds his arms; he says, "Well, we obviously

don't have the time to draw a complete picture of the situation in that period, but, briefly, the economy was on the verge of bankruptcy, we had a terrifying inflation rate, there was corruption everywhere, the government was run by incompetents whose only thought was to survive and to steal what they could while they could. And every sector of the government, every single source of jobs and money and information, had been shared out among the parties. They were everywhere. They were behind every bank and every newspaper and every art exhibition, behind every tailor and conductor and director and actor and reporter."

"What if somebody wasn't a member of any party?" Lise asks.

"Nothing," Ottavio says. "He simply never had any opportunity. He kept on with his activity, if he had one, and whatever he did cost him ten times the effort it should have. And anyone who, on the contrary, had a party card and some ambition could hope for the most brilliant and unmerited career. An architect who had never built a house could find himself commissioned to do an entire city, and be named president of some prestigious institution, mentioned on more and more occasions, sent abroad as a cultural envoy, invited to the Saturday-evening TV shows. There were no criteria of admission, no requirements. Having a party card and knowing how to maneuver were enough."

"What was the situation of television then, in general?" Lise asks, off camera, looking at Ted with nervous eyes.

Ottavio says, "Well, the private networks as a rule were each controlled by a party, and the state television by all the parties together. They had divided it up, like a piece of land divided into lots: each had taken a portion. The most incredible thing was the newscast. There was an old protectionist law on the books, which established that only the state television could broadcast news—the private stations couldn't. So all the parties had this even more limited terrain in which they had to act, those fifteen minutes they had to try to steal or bargain away from one another. The news became a kind of grotesque display case in which the faces and names of the politicians filed past constantly, on the flimsiest pretext. There were these melancholy television announcers seated at a desk, and they spent the time reading or reciting by heart declarations or summaries of the party representatives' speeches. In the background you saw the enlarged photograph of the politician in question, or some footage of him in Parliament or opening something or at a congress or a holiday celebration, and the announcer would report in a monotone the politician's words. And that way the words became remarkably lacking in any meaning at all."

"How did the politicians react to *Collisions*?" Lise asks.

"They were interested," Ottavio says. "I mean, they knew it was a program focusing on them: how could it fail to interest them? Their thirst for TV opportunities was beyond quenching. It's odd, because for years the politicians of this country had used TV with a certain distrust. It was theirs, naturally, and they exploited it as a propaganda machine: they allowed only the information they wanted, they filled the news programs with themselves even back then. But they tried always to appear in stylized images; they had themselves photo-

70

graphed in long shots, or only to the waist. They were frightened of closeups. They never appeared without a necktie; they hated to commit themselves or relax before the lens. Then a new generation of politicians came along that no longer had any fear of the TV cameras. Some began to seek greater exposure, have themselves filmed on Sundays at the beach while they were playing soccer, and they would have themselves asked questions about women, jealousy, money. And within a very short time the country was full of politicians discovering the pleasure of taking part in variety shows, in being politely persuaded to act or sing, put on costumes, make racy remarks. The old politicians became as eager as the new ones to get themselves seen—there wasn't enough space on television to contain them all. Until a moment before, they had been staid high priests in black and white; a moment later they were all character actors, dying for opportunities to become a star."

"So they immediately agreed to appear on *Collisions*?" Lise says.

"Yes," Ottavio says, "the minute Channel Eight began to test the audience reactions. In the space of a week there was a list for at least fifteen programs, ministers and party chairmen and vice-chairmen. They were just a bit puzzled by the fact that there was Macno instead of a more experienced person, but it didn't matter all that much to them. And Channel Eight wasn't some little unknown station, of course."

"Did they want any guarantees as far as the interviews were concerned?" Lise asks.

"Of course. The usual," Ottavio says. "They wanted

to agree on the questions beforehand, and know exactly everything that would be asked and said. Obviously, with a program going out live, nobody wanted to run any risks."

"What about Macno?" Lise says.

"Macno accepted the conditions almost immediately," Ottavio says. "The Channel Eight people were fairly surprised, I remember, because up till then he had defended his line with great insistence. But they all thought that this was the most realistic decision."

"And then what happened on the first broadcast?" Lise asks.

Ottavio turns and half-faces the camera; he says, "What happened was that Macno had agreed with Minister Tarminelli on all the questions, and when the broadcast was on the air he started asking different questions."

"How did it go?" Lise asks. "Were you there?"

"Of course, I was there in the studio," Ottavio says. "It was unbelievable. I think I'll always remember that half-hour. There was Tarminelli, sitting in his chair, stiff and sinister as he was, convinced that he was facing another opportunity for witty anecdotes and digressions, and suddenly he realized that Macno wasn't respecting any of the things they'd agreed on. I remember his *face*. I believe millions of viewers remember it, in fact. And Tarminelli was usually very clever. He had this technique of completely avoiding a question, skirting it, and moving off in an entirely different direction while still giving the impression of having answered. He had managed to remain in power for forty years without a break, moving from one Cabinet to another, from one ministry to another, surviving all his colleagues, getting out in time whenever one of them was swept away in a scandal. His trick was always to avoid questions, to evade them and digress. But it all depended on the questions, we realized that evening, and on who asked them."

"How did he react?" Lise says.

"At the beginning he was incredulous, mostly," Ottavio says. "Macno didn't give him a moment's respite, wouldn't let him move a centimeter from the heart of the question. Tarminelli would try to slip away, and Macno would interrupt him, repeat the question, approaching it from a different angle to block any avenue of escape. And the broadcast was *live*. Tarminelli couldn't say all right that's enough and get up and leave. He became more and more nervous, disjointed, until he was almost hysterical. During the last fifteen minutes of *Collisions* he ended up severely damaging his image as an intelligent, detached man: the image he had spent forty years creating for himself."

"And after the broadcast, what happened?" Lise says, staring at his lips, apprehensive at the thought that he might break off or become vague, rob his story of details.

Ottavio says, "Well, Tarminelli went off without saying a word, but it was clear that he was going to try to make everyone pay. The Channel Eight people didn't really know how to react. As journalism, the interview was a masterpiece; this country had never seen anything so tense and relentless and interesting. But from a political point of view, it was unacceptable; it broke all the rules of the game. I remember, when the mikes were turned off and Tarminelli had left, nobody said anything, nobody went over to Macno. There was this strange silence in the studio, as if we had all witnessed a crime or something of the sort."

73

"And then what happened, exactly?" Lise asks, tense.

"What happened was that Zefiri sent word that he wanted to see Macno in his office," Ottavio says. "I think he wanted to tell him he was fired and the program was cancelled. Zefiri was ambitious and prepared to take risks, but not to that degree. Tarminelli was minister of the interior and one of the most powerful politicians in the country, and if he had wanted to destroy Channel Eight he would surely have succeeded."

"So then what?" Lise says.

"Then things went the way we all know," Ottavio says. "While Macno was waiting in the corridor outside Zefiri's office, all the phones at Channel Eight were ringing— there were calls and calls, from people who were enthusiastic or furious but tremendously involved in any case. Within an hour *Collisions* had become the most popular program in the country, and Macno had gained an immense following. The television people were beside themselves."

"Why?" Lise says.

"Well," Ottavio says, "until then everyone had insisted that the television audience wanted mirror images, people in whom they could identify their own weaknesses and faults; and suddenly Macno showed that it wasn't true. He showed that what the audience wanted was to see itself as *better*. There was a terrific thirst for great qualities, for sincere feelings, in this country where cynicism and pettiness seemed so widespread. You could say that what Macno did was bring a big-screen character to the small screen, and then into real life."

"So Zefiri decided to go on with *Collisions?*" Lise asks.

"I believe *nobody* would have refused ten million viewers," Ottavio says. "Zefiri must have thought that at that point the risk was worth running, and, further, that there was surely some way of reducing it, even though today we know there wasn't. So he went ahead with the other programs, until the situation became intolerable. What seems oddest today is that the politicians continued to accept the invitation to participate. It's comprehensible only if you remember their attitude at the time, their terrible eagerness to be seen on television. And they were all convinced that they would prove themselves smarter than Tarminelli."

"How did the opposition parties behave with Macno?" Lise says, trying to pick the right question from the many that press into her mind.

"In the beginning, naturally, they tried to devour him," Ottavio says. "They flattered him, they said he was doing an incredible job, that they would help him and support him and defend him. They offered him party cards, seats in Parliament. But it didn't take them long to discover that Macno was against them as much as he was against the parties in the coalition. Which was really inconceivable at that time. To be against a party was conceivable only if you were acting from the positions of another party. If you were against Catholic Unity then you had to be a Communist, or vice versa. That way, everything was legitimate and identifiable. But Macno said that the choice a voter had was like the choice of a woman facing seven possible husbands, each one full of loathsome faults, and she had to pick the one that horrified her least. So the Communists then began saying Macno was a Fascist, the Fascists said he was a Communist, the center parties called him an unprincipled opportunist. The fact is that nobody knew what side to attack him from. Macno totally eluded their logic. It was as if he came from the moon."

"Then what?" Lise says, leaning toward him.

"Nothing," Ottavio says. "*Collisions* went on for the rest of the installments, and when the parties finally realized what was happening and forced Zefiri to cancel the program after the interview with Adamo Tuorli, it was too late. Nobody imagined that television could have such an effect. They had played with it for years like neurotic children, never thinking that someone might arrive who knew how to use it the way Macno did."

Lise says, "Did Macno have a specific political plan when he started working on *Collisions*? Did you discuss it?"

"No," Ottavio says. "We discussed the political implications of a program focusing on encounters with political figures, naturally." He looks to one side, with a tense smile. He says, "Macno had very specific ideas on many subjects, and he realized the possible consequences of what he was doing, but he didn't have a plan. At least not at the start. He began to work it out later. After the first installments of *Collisions*."

Lise says, "What sort of work did you do together for the programs, exactly?"

"We discussed the shape the various subjects should be given," Ottavio says. "I mean, in terms of television language. My contribution was only technical; the rest Macno knew himself, very well. He had a talent for instinctive communication, quite extraordinary."

"How do you mean instinctive?" Lise says.

Ottavio adjusts the lapel of his jacket. "He could sense

the moods of the audience, and *feel* the extent of its participation. He was sitting there, in the cold silence of the television studio, and he gave you the impression that he had a real audience in front of him. He could sense beyond the cameramen and the light men, the cameras and the lights and the wires and the tripods. He had this extraordinary ability." He looks to one side, he looks at the camera. He says, "He still has it, naturally." He straightens up in an attitude that says end of interview, stretches his thin lips in a smile.

Lise asks him, "How did Macno react to the enormous attention paid to him after *Collisions*? I mean, from a personal point of view?"

"Well, I believe you should ask him that," Ottavio says. He smiles again, tense and polite. He looks into the camera once more; he looks at Lise, says to her, "Very well."

Lise says to him, "I have a few more questions I'd like to ask you." She turns to look at Ted, who has already stopped filming; he has set the camera on his knee.

Ottavio gives his watch a rapid glance, says, "I'd be happy to go on, but unfortunately I must run." He smiles and says, "Frankly, when I came here I wasn't thinking of such a serious interview. I thought we'd chat a moment, but you've drawn me into an analytical re-examination." He goes to shake Ted's hand; he says, "In any case, if you really want to, we can continue another time. I imagine you'll have to stay here a few more days for the interview with Macno anyway." He kisses Lise's hand, opens the door.

Lise follows him into the corridor; she says to him, "Do you think Macno will really give us the interview, sooner or later?"

"Absolutely," Ottavio says. "He certainly isn't some-one who makes a promise and then doesn't keep it."

Lise says, "Let's hope not." She looks at his profile as he looks to the end of the corridor. She says to him, "Anyway, thank you very much, Mr. Larici."

"Not at all," Ottavio says. "I enjoyed it." He smiles almost openly this time; he says, "Perhaps we can use first names. As you must have seen, here we're usually very informal."

"Fine," Lise says, thinking it's not really a matter of genuine informality but, rather, a subtle formality com-posed of nuances and hints and degrees of smiling.

Ottavio says, "Now I really must run. But I hope we'll see each other again soon."

"See you later, then," Lise says.

"Soon," Ottavio says, his feet itching, though he is polite. He waves a brief good-bye, then goes off rapidly down the corridor.

Lise turns back toward the private study, where two guards are motionless at the door.

NINE

Lise and Ted are playing croquet on the lawn with a ballerina from Milan, a young Australian ethnologist, and a Yugoslav acrobat with a shaved head. The early-afternoon sun is hot; the park silent, suspended. Guards and waiters glide along the laurel hedges. The wooden sound of the croquet mallets striking the maple balls reverberates against the white walls of the palace.

A heavyset character in a gray jacket comes out of a French window, crosses the lawn, comes to whisper something to the Australian ethnologist. She shakes her head; she points her finger at Lise, six meters farther on.

The heavyset character comes over to Lise, hands her a little white envelope.

Lise puts down the croquet mallet, opens the little envelope with nervous fingers. The note, written in a strong hand, says, *If you want, the bearer of this note can bring you here. M.*

Ted smartly strikes a ball, sends it rolling a long way, beyond a hoop. He says, "Not bad, huh?" to the Yugoslav. He turns to look at Lise with the note in her hand; he says to her, "What is it?"

"Nothing," Lise says, clasping the note in her fingers. She signals to the heavyset character that she agrees.

"What do you mean, nothing?" Ted says, coming over. He shifts his gaze from Lise to the heavyset character, who withdraws a few steps, his eyes vague. Ted reaches out, tries to open Lise's fist, says, "Let me have a look."

Lise hides her hand behind her back; she says, "It's for the interview. I have to go and talk with somebody." Her cheeks are flushed, her eyes bright; she is ready to dart off.

"Somebody who?" Ted says, slowly.

"Somebody. I'll tell you later," Lise says. She gives him a reassuring sign, waves to the others; she steps back toward the heavyset character.

"Who the hell are you going to see?" Ted says, uncertain whether to follow her or not. "Ottavio Larici?"

"I'll tell you later. Don't act so suspicious," Lise says. She turns, follows the heavyset character toward the palace.

Ted looks around. The Yugoslav, leaning on his mallet, says, "Well?" Ted looks at Lise: already close to the

French window. He shrugs, again studies his position in the game.

Lise follows the heavyset character into the palace, across the entrance hall, along a corridor, down a stairway, into a big garage. There is a trim white car with dark windows. The heavyset character opens the rear door; Lise gets in.

The car glides along the gravel driveway, slows down beneath the eyes of the guards who open the gate; it comes out into the road, picks up speed. The garden wall, the great crowns of the trees flow by.

Lise takes the note out of the little crumpled envelope. She rereads it with rapid eyes: two or three possible interpretations arise one after the other. She rereads it more slowly; she lingers on the individual words, on their relationship to the words that follow and precede them. She rereads it at least ten times; and each time she is less sure that this is an invitation or a concession, an impulse or a routine message. She sniffs it, but it seems to have no smell; she puts it back in the little envelope, clasps it in her fingers. She looks out: a fragment of ancient temple kept standing, as a traffic island.

The car crosses the center of the city, darts along jammed streets. The driver exploits the tiniest free spaces, slaloms, accelerates in lanes reserved for buses. When he can't find a way open, he turns on an intermittent siren; the other cars huddle together, side to side and bumper to bumper, to allow him to pass. The trim white car cuts intersections, crosses on the red light as traffic cops wave it on with their little sticks; it runs down a pedestrian street, three strollers fling themselves to one side to avoid being knocked down. Lise grips the handle, looks often out of the window, which softens the brusque movements and muffles the sound of the horn, the squeal of the brakes, and the roar of accelerations.

The car climbs up a street flanked by shops with great windows where elegant women are walking past and whole parties of Japanese tourists. It turns left, climbs another, narrower street between two lines of cars parked half on the sidewalks, brakes in front of a little door with a metal blind drawn down. The driver presses a button on the dashboard; the blind descends, disappears. The car enters, goes down a pebbled ramp, proceeds on a level, stops at a second blind. The second blind is lowered; the car goes ahead for thirty meters, stops. The driver jumps down, comes and opens the door for Lise.

Lise looks around the basement garage, sniffs the odor of crankcase oil and gasoline and cellar damp. There is another parked car, with dark windows like the one she arrived in. Lise follows the driver to the door of an elevator. The driver opens it, stands outside.

The elevator rises without buttons, slow and silent. Lise looks at herself in the mirror; she moistens a fingertip, runs it over the corners of her eyes. She tries to slow the beating of her heart. The elevator stops.

Palmario says "Good afternoon" to her in a padded antechamber. He leads her toward a door, opens it, withdraws.

Lise walks between the walls of a corridor, on a pale wool carpeting that muffles her footsteps. She looks in at a door: a little kitchen, with a low refrigerator and a sink and a stove. There is an arched window, and on the other side of the glass a tendril of Virginia creeper.

She goes to the end of the corridor, turns the corner: a living room lighted by a great window. The furniture is scant and blond and low, of fir and white fabric; there is a grand piano beside the window. The window opens onto a terrace, and standing on the terrace is Macno, who turns around.

Lise crosses the living room, goes out into the intense light of the afternoon.

Macno looks into her eyes as he approaches, says "How are you?" He is wearing a pale-blue shirt with full sleeves; behind him a bougainvillea climbs on lines of nylon, forming a violet-and-green curtain bleached by the sun.

"Fine, thanks," Lise says with an apprehensive smile, stopping a meter and a half from him.

They look at each other over this distance, without shaking hands or exchanging other gestures of greeting. There are no sounds or movements.

Then Macno points to the bougainvillea, says, "You see?" Lise comes forward on his right, so they are side by side and not a centimeter closer than before. And beyond the climbing leaves there is the city: the roofs of reddish tiles, the flat roofs of cement, the pink terraces green with potted palmettos and honeysuckle and jasmine, the cylindrical tanks, the glassed mansards, the cubes of masonry, the edges and the white cornices, the dormers, the railings, the arches of the windows, the little columns, the big air conditioners, the bushy green of the private gardens, the gray channels of the streets, where slow lines of automobiles pass, the ancient marbles and the arches and the obelisks and the domes, the irregular expanse that spreads and spreads in shades of yellow and pale orange to the faint greening of the hills where Macno's palace stands. Lise looks beyond the leaves and the bracts of bougainvillea, absorbed in the vibration of traffic that rises from below. She says, "It's incredible."

"Yes," Macno says. He comes closer, extends his hand, and removes two or three dry bracts.

Lise waits for him to say something else: turned toward him, with one hand on her gray silk skirt. She feels vague and weak, lacking any sense of humor. The city throbs behind her; the late-afternoon light is still too strong.

Macno doesn't say anything; he grazes the leaves with an air of concentration.

Lise turns to look again at the city, casting her eyes around in search of a hold. She points a finger, says, "There's the pension where we were staying. At least, I think that's it." She looks, uncertain, and suddenly she thinks of how far away her life before meeting Macno is, how unclear, separated from her life now by a space far larger than the days that have gone by.

Macno raises his eyes to her; he says, "What was it like, the pension?"

"I believe there are better," Lise says with a smile. She runs her hand through her hair, she says, "The landlady was fat and morbidly curious, and the stairway always smelled of cabbage and fried lamb."

"Roast," Macno says. He goes on looking at the bougainvillea, he says, "Years ago I lived in a pension like that, too. They roast it in the oven, the lamb."

"Ah," Lise says. She half-closes her eyes, looks at the sun, which has already started descending on the city.

Macno leans on the wrought-iron railing. He looks down, says, "And what do you think of this city?"

"Ah, that it's beautiful," Lise says, impulsive as a tourist.

Macno continues looking down, with just the shadow of a smile on his lips.

Lise is filled with anger at the thought of having seemed so superficial and naïve to him; she says, "And what do you think of it?"

Macno says, "Now, then, where shall I begin?" as if he were reluctantly submitting to the opening of an interview. He looks with apparent interest at a gray cat walking along the eave of a roof.

"I don't know," Lise says, puzzled. She doesn't really know whether to wait or to change the subject or to go away. She continues looking at him from one side: the profile familiar to millions of people who at this moment haven't the slightest idea where he is.

Macno says, "It's so vulgar, and pandering, and dishonest, and unruffled in spite of everything. It's like the people who live in it; or perhaps the people are like the city. And you see the sun, the color the plaster walls take on, how open the space is and also how stifling." He goes and picks two kumquats from a potted tree; he hands one to Lise, sniffs the other with a pensive look. He says, "At one point I even thought I could change it, but the idea was ridiculous. It's a thousand times easier for the city to change me."

Lise is looking at him, in silence, almost frightened at the thought of having inspired such negative reflections in him. She gnaws her little fruit, with its bitter rind.

Macno puts one hand on his neck; he says, "Everything becomes so slow here, so terribly complicated. It's

85

a city that absorbs everything, and manages to lose everything along the way."

Lise looks at him close, and it seems to her impossible to understand completely the light in his eyes, the color in his voice.

Macno still looks down, silent for almost a minute. He turns toward her; he says, "Have you heard the *language* they speak in this city? The lazy, cynical way they chop off words three-quarters spoken and stick one to the other, overladen with accents and drawled out so that they give the exact same meaning to whatever sentence they may compose?" He looks at Lise's hair, her keen eyes; he says to her, "But perhaps to you, from outside, it seems a musical language, full of life and imagination."

Lise smiles awkwardly; she says, "No . . ." She turns to face the sun, now almost without strength, low over the city, which reflects it in shades of warm yellow. There is a breath of wind, rising.

Macno sees her shiver slightly; he says to her, "If you're cold, we can go inside."

"I'm not cold," Lise says.

Macno says, "But we can go inside anyway."

They go inside. Macno slides the thick glass; he shuts it carefully. He crosses the sitting room.

Lise follows his movements, and she seems to be perceiving them without any perspective. She looks at the grand piano, a white sofa; she runs her hand through her hair.

Macno goes and turns on a stereo on a shelf; he pulls out a little record, sticks it into the scanner. Some marimba music spreads through the room: liquid, rippling in repeated rhythms. Lise looks around in search of clues: a can of colored pastels on a little table.

Macno takes a few steps with his hand on his hip, looks around as if he were disappointed by the space. He looks at Lise, says, "It's not a big apartment. There's only one other room." He points in the direction of the other room. He says, "The ridiculous thing is that to have it we had to take all six floors of the building. And we can't even get into them, because the elevator only stops here."

"I saw," Lise says, also thinking of something quite different. They are six meters apart, divided by a few low pieces of furniture, and every movement seems to cost an effort: every word and change of expression. Lise strikes with two fingers a little curtain of mother-of-pearl discs that break up the sunset light and touch one another with watery sounds like a xylomarimba's. She takes a few steps; she looks at the walls. There is a little Matisse in a narrow frame: a naked woman on a sofa, drawn by a single line of pencil. Lise observes it with expanded attention, lingers on the curves.

Macno comes to her side; he also looks. He breathes silently at her left.

Lise follows the sign of the pencil, and the whole left part of her body feels the slight distance that separates her from Macno.

Macno turns toward her; he says, "When I wrote you that note I wanted you already here."

"Yes?" Lise says now without any nonchalance, with her heart beating irregularly.

"Yes," Macno says. "I didn't have any wish to wait for you."

They look into each other's eyes at twenty centimeters' distance, the tension becomes compressed. Then
Macno extends his hand and puts it on Lise's face; she
slides toward him: pulled by an undertow.

He holds her in strong arms; she loses the sense of her
own outlines. They kiss, and she feels only the flow of
energy, the magnetic warmth that lengthens her breathing and makes the liquids of which she is composed circulate feverishly. He comes forward, she goes backward.
He goes backward, she follows him. Every swaying moves
them farther from the difficulty of gestures and the difficulty of expressions, the difficulty of organized thoughts;
it moves them farther and farther from the search for
balance, from the tension required by the slightest form
of behavior. Lise and Macno hold each other until they
are so close and mingled that neither of the two would
be able to see himself from the outside any more. They
embrace for perhaps five minutes, and nothing in the room
or beyond the room has any further meaning.

Macno slowly detaches himself, looks at her. He reaches
out, and his hand takes whole seconds to arrive at her
hair, to uncover one ear, small and shapely. Lise narrows
her eyes. He runs his fingers over her neck, along the
curve of her shoulder, down her side to the indentation
of her waist, the full curve of her hip. He comes back
up with light fingertips; he smiles when she reopens her
eyes.

"What are you laughing at?" she says, with a vague
voice.

"I'm not laughing," Macno says. He rumples her hair
with his hand.

"But you were smiling," Lise says, tilting her head. "What were you smiling at?"

"I don't know. At you," he says slowly.

"Why?" Lise says. There is a childish and eager light in her eyes.

Macno smiles again, strokes her temple. He says, "Because you are very pretty, and have very light skin, and are also a bit crazy—to come here, climbing over the wall."

Lise looks at his eyes and his lips; she says in an insulted tone, "What do you mean, pretty?" She isn't completely sure, either; and the difficulties have only moved off.

Macno says, "I didn't mean it in the sense of *pretty*. And, anyway, words never mean what they should. Perhaps we shouldn't even talk. I only wanted to say that I like you a lot."

"Really?" Lise says.

"Yes," Macno says.

There is an electronic *beep beep beep*. Macno raises his wrist, looks at his watch, says, "Oh, Jesus Christ." He looks at Lise and the difficulties are returning, coming back to possess every movement. He says, "I have to be somewhere in ten minutes."

She turns to look at the window, giving onto a violet-red sky streaked by darker lines.

Macno looks at the floor; he says, "I'm sorry. I'd forgotten all about it."

"It doesn't matter," Lise says; and they are again distant, separated by low furniture, concerned with the way they are standing.

Macno goes and turns off the stereo: the marimba music disappears, as if it had never existed. He looks at Lise as she crosses the room. He says to her, "And we didn't even talk about the interview."

"Next time," Lise says.

"Yes," Macno says. He looks at her for another instant; he leads her to the corridor.

In the antechamber Palmario is ready at the door of the elevator. All three go down, without saying anything or looking at one another.

They come out into the garage, where the two chauffeurs are waiting beside the white cars with dark windows. Macno turns to Lise, says to her: "So long, then. We'll talk tomorrow." The chauffeurs open the doors with simultaneous movements.

Lise says, "All right." And Macno has already got into the car; the car has already disappeared into the tunnel.

TEN

Macno, followed by Ester, comes into the little room, crosses it to the long console with the three small screens opposite which Ottavio and the cutter are seated. "Well?" he says, as his recorded voice comes from the loudspeakers, mixed with noises of the crowd.

Ottavio turns; he says, "We've done about half, more or less."

The cutter gestures a respectful greeting; he stops the tapes, the soundtrack.

Macno says, "Go ahead."

The cutter hesitates, his fingers on the buttons. On

the first screen Macno is motionless, microphone in hand; on the others, shots of motionless crowd. Ottavio says, "We'll take it from the last words."

The cutter taps on the keys; the three tapes reverse fast; they stop, begin running in the right direction again. On the first screen Macno walks across the platform, in one of the less overwhelming passages of the Third Anniversary speech. On the second is the crowd assembled to listen to it, but it isn't the same as the crowd of the speech; it is many other crowds dug up from different situations and times and moods, with different expressions and sounds and ways of moving, broken up into a succession of levels and frames. On the third screen the shots of Macno and the crowd seem to alternate: every sentence with its vocal reactions, every gesture with its gestures of response.

Macno turns to look at Ester, who stares at the little screens with fascinated eyes. At the door Uto Rumi approaches the counter with short steps, a generic smile on his lips.

"This one," Ottavio says to the cutter, pointing to a fragment of intent crowd passing on the central screen.

The cutter works at the keys with rapid fingers, as if his activity were something completely natural: he runs the tapes forward and backward, stops them, starts them again from the beginning, shifts images from one screen to another, alert to signals from Ottavio. As the crowd shots gradually appear on the third screen, he brushes the controls with his fingertips, adjusts the color and the light so that the shots are uniform, blends the fragments into a homogeneous whole. And the voices, the shouts, the applause take on the same consistency, balanced to make up a constant soundtrack under and between and after the words of Macno.

Uto Rumi shifts his eyes from one screen to another, standing with his hands behind his back, between Macno and Ester. His breathing is laborious, as if he had climbed some flights of stairs before entering. Macno looks at the faces of the crowd, trying to figure out to which speech they had reacted originally. Ottavio says "This one," or "The first"; the cutter taps rapidly on the keys; fragment by fragment, the images are composed into credible sequences. On the first screen Macno speaks and goes back and repeats the same phrase fifteen times in a row, and at the fifteenth the faces on the third screen reflect the meaning of his every word, and from comprehension they pass to approbation, from approbation to enthusiasm; they break into smiles, shouts, gestures of frantic exuberance.

Ottavio turns on his stool, says to Macno, "What do you think?"

"It seems ridiculous to me," Macno says, his arms folded.

"I tell you it's very natural, on the contrary," Ottavio says. "Nothing is forced."

Macno says, "But they were on the verge of *booing* me, for Christ's sake. You can't make them yell with enthusiasm now. It's ridiculous."

Ottavio signals to the cutter to go back. The cutter rewinds the tape; the sequence runs again, with the crescendo of the crowd on Macno's words. Ottavio says, "It's not at all ridiculous. Look. It works."

"I don't give a damn if it works," Macno says. "You

93

can do it for some Saturday-night variety show, but not for a speech." He turns to look at Ester and says, "Don't you agree?"

Ester says, "I don't know"; she looks at the images frozen on the screens.

Macno looks at Uto Rumi; he says, "Don't you agree it's grotesque?"

Uto Rumi says, "Look, it's hard to say, because on the one hand you're absolutely right, if you're thinking that the reactions shouldn't go beyond the natural reactions of the home viewers; but on the other hand it seems to me that Ottavio is right, since it's true that the viewer reads on the screen extreme reactions, ignoring nuances, and a generically favorable face certainly isn't contagious the way an enthusiastic face is, and the purpose of having a live speech is, in fact, to create an effect of contagion—"

"All right, all right," Macno interrupts him. "In any case, I have no desire to transform the speech into a farce."

Ottavio says, "In my opinion it's not that at all, but if you don't like it, we'll change it. We'll put what you want."

"Yes," Macno says, "but don't say it in that tone, like somebody indulging a caprice."

"I didn't say it was a caprice," Ottavio says in a patient voice. "I said we'll put what you want."

"Yes, but you have that tone, as if you were forced to humor a poor lunatic."

"That's not true," Ottavio says. "If you want to think that, then go ahead; but you know very well it's not true."

"But it is true," Macno says, raising his voice. "And I know very well that you think I no longer have any idea of how to use television, or at least that my idea is still two years out of date and I'm losing my grip on things. All because I won't let you put in people yelling and waving their arms every time I say boo, and teen-age girls fainting every time I smile."

Ottavio stands up, says, "Listen, I'm not having any fun at all, playing with this stuff." His voice also rises, loses definition. He says, "It's my job, that's all. I'm only trying to do it the best I can."

"No, you're having a lot of fun," Macno says to him. His voice can rise without any trace of hoarseness or shrillness; it rises clear and full of color. He says, "You have so much fun that you lose your head completely every time you're there with that stupid toy. You don't even think any more of the purpose of what you're doing, only of *how* to do it. You think only of doing a fine professional job, mixing the sounds, and toning the colors, and cutting the images so that nobody can see even a hint of a splice. You don't give a damn about what this speech actually means; that's not your business, because you're only a communications expert, the best on the market, right?"

"Listen, Macno," Ottavio says, his fists clenched, his lips thin and pale. "It's not my fault that the people at the speech didn't applaud, and didn't even seem convinced. It would be a lot easier to use the original footage, if we only could. It's not my fault that the original footage is so disappointing that it would depress the whole country if we broadcast it as it is."

Macno is motionless; Ottavio is motionless. Ester and Uto Rumi are motionless. The cutter is motionless at his screens, his fingers still on the keys. For a few seconds there isn't a single movement or sound in the little room with its cold light.

Ottavio adjusts one cuff.

Ester chews her lip.

Uto Rumi says, "Now, let's not start saying things that nobody thinks. We know very well that at this moment we're all tired and—"

"There's no point in your playing Father Peacemaker now," Macno says to him. He casts an absent look over the walls; he goes toward the door. Ester follows him out.

Ottavio looks at Uto Rumi with eyes still glistening and slightly reddened by his tension. Neither of the two says anything. Their eyes go to the three screens on the console: to the frozen images.

E L E V E N

The sun comes in through the window and Lise looks at herself in the closet mirror, seeking some trace of what happened yesterday. She observes her lips closely, runs her fingers over her cheeks, her neck. Her thoughts revolve, slow and vague, halted and accelerated by sudden palpitations. She stands for a long time before the open closet, indecisive; she picks a short dress, mauve-colored, and slips it on.

She goes into the bath and slowly applies her makeup. She tries to remember the way Macno said to her, "We'll talk tomorrow." She tries to go back to his words as if they were recorded on a tape: she listens to them one by one, and his way of pronouncing them. They seem to her a definite appointment, with no margin for the unexpected or any change of mind, and immediately afterward, on the contrary, they constitute a vague sentence, without any precise reference: "tomorrow," only another way of saying "in the near future," or even "sooner or later." She goes back to two seconds before the sentence: to Macno who turns toward her in the basement garage and parts his lips. She goes back again and again to that moment; she sees it in slow motion in order to read, in that parting of the lips, the meaning of the words that follow. She draws a fine line of shadow around her eyes. She goes further back: to herself and Macno not looking at each other in the elevator; to Macno in the sitting room saying to her, "I'm sorry"; to Macno looking at his watch; to Macno trying to explain to her what he means when he says pretty; to her and Macno breaking from the embrace; to her and Macno breathing very close, mingled and almost without thoughts; to the way they stood in the sitting room before embracing. She takes a pinch of red powder from a little box, faintly colors her cheeks.

She comes out of the bath, walks on her heels, seeing nothing of the room, in her head the same sequence of movements now being rewound from the end toward the beginning. She would like to talk about it with someone but doesn't know with whom; and the less that whom comes to her mind, the more she would like to talk. She takes a cassette at random from the rack, thrusts it into the video; on the screen a group of Australian aborigines appears, taking turns sucking water with a straw from an

emu egg. The soundtrack is nothing but drums. Somebody knocks at the door.

Lise runs; she slows down the last two steps. She says,
"Who is it," opens the door, filled with eagerness.

It is Ted in t-shirt and shorts, sweating, red in the
face, still breathless from jogging. He says "Hey" and
immediately comes in.

"Hi," Lise says to him, still at the door.

Ted takes a few steps, his hands on his hips; heavy in
his thick springy shoes. He says, "Have you decided to
give up working out for good and just let yourself go?"

"I was too sleepy this morning," Lise says.

Ted looks around, says, "Why? Did you go carry on
somehow with that killer type who brought you the message yesterday afternoon?"

"It was work, idiot," Lise says, looking him in the eyes
an instant. "It was to talk about the interview."

"It was?" Ted says. From a shelf he takes a painted
wooden duck, observes it with feigned attention. He says,
"And who with, if I may ask?"

"With Ottavio Larici," Lise says hastily, stumbling
slightly over the name.

"And what did he want to say to you?" Ted says,
looking at the duck's tail.

"Mm," Lise says. "He wanted to discuss the questions
to ask Macno, and the interview in general."

"And you talked about that all afternoon?" Ted says.

"Yes," Lise says. She looks up at him, says, "What is
this? The third degree?"

Ted places the duck on the shelf; he says, "No, nothing. It's just that Ottavio Larici was here after you went

off. I saw him downstairs in the tea room; he actually told me to say hello to you."

Lise looks at him, alarm in her eyes; she says, "What?"

"All right," Ted says. "It doesn't matter. You're free to do what you like. Only there's no point in your telling me a lot of crap."

"I'm not telling you crap," Lise says. On the video the sound of drumming continues, without any great variations of rhythm. Lise says, "And don't start playing the jealous husband again, please."

"I'm not playing anything," Ted says, with a hurt look. "But, seeing that we're here to do a job together, allow me to worry also about what happens to you."

"All right," Lise says. "Don't get hurt feelings now." She looks at the screen, where the group of aborigines is walking in Indian file across an expanse of sand.

Ted says, "Anyway, apart from what you're doing, which quite rightly doesn't concern me, what the hell is going on with the interview? I mean, what with one thing and another we've been here ten days, and so far we haven't achieved anything."

"Well, to begin with, we have the stuff with Larici," Lise says. She presses the remote controls, silences the TV sounds.

Ted says, "But Ottavio Larici isn't news. He's a ghost; nobody knows who he is."

"But we've got him," Lise says. "And we should do the interview with Macno within the next few days. He said yes to us, so we can count on it. He's not a man who makes a promise and then doesn't keep it."

"How do you know?" Ted says. "Everybody who knows him says just the opposite. I talked again with

New York, and Phil says he knew it all along—he was sure that at the last minute the character would change his mind and wouldn't show up."

"Phil doesn't know him at all," Lise says. "He's never seen Macno in his life."

"No," Ted says. "But he knows a lot of people who've had dealings with him, and it was the same story with all of them. We're likely to end up seeming two naïve idiots who fool themselves that they can pull off a trick where everybody else has failed. Yesterday evening I talked with Gloria Hedges, and she says she knew it, too. She didn't want to say anything before, so as not to spoil our fun, but she knew we'd never manage the interview."

"Listen: Gloria Hedges is a hyena," Lise says. "You said so yourself. She'll be happy if things go wrong for us."

Ted pulls up one sock and says, "Anyway, we'll see. I hope we don't have to stay here two months. I'll be happy if we just bring off the interview; that's the only thing I'm interested in."

"We'll do it, Ted," Lise says. "I'm sure we'll do it."

"I hope so," Ted says. He goes toward the door.

Lise follows him, trying to catch his glance. She says to him, "Now where are you going? Are you angry?"

"No," Ted says, opening the door. "I'm going for a shower. We'll meet later."

"Okay," Lise says. She shuts the door, takes a few hesitant steps in the room, looks at the screen, where the aborigines are building a brushwood hut. She turns off the video, leaves the room, goes down to the ground floor.

She looks out of a French window onto the garden, and a strong wind is rising, dragging great gray clouds to cover the sun. The greens of the lawn and the trees are darkening; the shadows dissolve. She goes back inside, looks through the glass at the clouds growing thicker and thicker, breaking into rain, which falls heavily on the park, on the gray water of the lake, which vibrates under the percussion of the furious drops. Lise watches, filled with anxiety and nostalgia; she feels someone touch her arm.

It is Ottavio, neatly shaven, hair combed; smooth and elegant. He says to her, "How's everything, Lise?"

"Hi," Lise says, slightly disturbed by his bergamot cologne.

Ottavio points outside, says, "It really is the end of May, isn't it?"

"Yes," Lise says.

He makes a gesture, says, "Would you like to have some tea with me? We could talk for a moment."

"All right," Lise says. She follows him toward one of the little rooms, her thoughts still very vague.

They sit on a sofa by a window, looking for a few seconds at different points in the room. From outside comes the rushing sound of the rain. Ottavio says, "Well, how are things going?" His tone is perhaps just a bit condescending, but very alert.

"Oh, all right," Lise says.

Ottavio signals a waitress, who comes over at once; he asks Lise, "What'll you have?"

"Nothing, I believe," Lise says.

"Two Lapsang Souchong," Ottavio says. The waitress slips away.

They remain for a few moments in silence. Lise looks for a comfortable position so as not to be at his side, as if on a train seat.

Ottavio says, "Listen, I've spoken again with Macno about the interview."

"Ah," Lise says: leaning toward him.

"Yes," Ottavio says. "I told him what you mentioned to me the other time: that you'd like to do something very informal, a kind of chat, in which he would speak very freely about himself."

"What did he say?" Lise says.

"Macno agrees absolutely," Ottavio says. "He likes the idea very much. Now it's only a question of setting the right moment, because I imagine it will also take more than an hour, as we had said before. It will take two, perhaps."

"Yes, two hours would be better," Lise says, without the slightest idea of how long would really be necessary. "Two would be perfect."

The waitress returns, sets the cups and teapot on the table.

Ottavio says, "Fine, now we'll check Macno's engagements for the coming week, and as soon as there's half a morning or half an afternoon not too clogged up, we'll fix the time."

"Okay," Lise says, trying to assume a professional tone. She tries to imagine herself doing the interview: the questions and the tone of the questions.

Ottavio pours her tea with a perfect movement. He says, "In the meantime I've thought of something that might perhaps interest you. I don't know if you've heard: we have a very complete tape library here, with all of Macno's speeches, all his TV appearances before he became president: practically speaking, everything he's done on video till now."

"I didn't know," Lise says. "I mean, I imagined it, but I didn't know."

"Yes," Ottavio says, pouring himself tea. "There is this very complete archive, and no journalist has ever been able to stick his nose into it. Of course, everybody is familiar with the speeches and the recent things, but there's material that nobody remembers—the first videos, the first installments of *Collisions*, and other material."

"Ah," Lise says. The downpour outside softens, dies away in a light rustle of drops on the grass.

Ottavio says, "Anyway, I thought that if you're interested, you could take a look. It might give you some more ideas for your interview. And in any case, since no reporters have been allowed to see it, I thought it might be worthwhile."

"It's interesting, of course," Lise says eagerly. "When could it be seen?"

Ottavio takes a sip of tea; he says, "Why, tomorrow morning, even. I'll try to find a free hour so we can start looking at something." He drinks another sip, sets the cup on the table.

"Fine," Lise says.

Ottavio stands up, says, "I'm sorry I have to leave you, but it's very late." He moves around the table and comes to kiss her hand. He lets his eyes pause for half a second on hers, with a quick brightness that Lise can't decipher. He says, "See you tomorrow, then." He goes toward the door: solid shoulders, sure of even his slightest movement.

Lise watches him go out, and thinks that he reminds her of a naval officer she saw once in a costume movie.

He has the same inner indestructibility, barely veneered by the elegance of his movements and expressions. She takes a sip of tea, lukewarm though it is now. She stands up, looks out of the window: the clouds are fading toward white, shredded by the wind, to reveal patches of intense blue.

T W E L V E

Macno climbs into the pale-blue helicopter. From inside he watches Dunnell bend over, his mouse-colored hair disheveled by the wind from the blades. Macno watches him climb up awkwardly with the help of Palmario, come and sit at his right, pull in his knees, contract in his fear of the flight. The helicopter rises above the lawn, above the formal half of the park, above the white palace between the two halves, above the hill on which park and palace stand; above the pink and yellowish and gray city for which the hill is only one pale-green patch among others.

Dunnell looks down, his hands clutching the sides of the seat. From time to time he takes an apprehensive look at the movements of the pilot, at the gauges and the luminous indicators.

Macno observes his sharp profile, his rumpled hair. He says to him, "Henry, this speech isn't coming to me. It doesn't work." He almost has to shout to cover the noise of the engine, in spite of the soundproofing panels and the armor.

Dunnell continues to look down, rigid. He says, "What do you mean, it won't work?"

"Stop looking down," Macno says. "We won't fall, I swear."

Dunnell raises his head, looks at Macno with eyes that are hesitant behind the glasses. He says, "Yesterday I saw the footage from the last time."

Macno stares at his lips, waiting for more words. He says, "Lousy, wasn't it?"

"No," Dunnell says. "It isn't lousy at all. Even if it certainly isn't the kind of speech that would be needed now. The two questions are separate. One is what you say, the other is the effect that what you say should have."

"Namely?" Macno says, tense.

Dunnell casts an apprehensive glance below; he says, "If you want to know what I think, I think this is one of your finest speeches, actually. I can't remember one more sincere, and also *strong* in a certain sense, closer to the essence of things. On the other hand, from a political point of view, it's surely the least opportune. Maybe it's even disastrous. I can fully understand why Ottavio and Uto are distraught."

They pass over a great white dome that looks onto a

square flanked by columns. In the streets around it, lines of automobiles move in jerks, like little columns of mercury in glass tubes.

Macno says, "I don't really know what it is. I've done four, and it always comes out the same. Every time, I feel I already have in my head all the words to present every problem in the most favorable light, to play down the obstacles, bring the prospects closer, touch the right keys and make the springs jump, and when I'm there on the platform, in front of the crowd, who wants to hear exactly what I have in my head, ready to be aroused and be carried away by the simple confirmation of their expectations, I come out and say something entirely different. It's ridiculous, because while I'm speaking I know very well that this is the most mistaken and counterproductive key, and a public speech can't be made in those terms; I know I'll disappoint everybody and will screw up the mechanisms of identification, and I go ahead all the same. And it isn't a desire for sincerity, at least I don't think it is. I don't know what it is. Maybe it's only a kind of self-destructive impulse."

Dunnell looks down below; he says, "Of course, you always manage to be so clear, damn it." He says this in the tone of a surprised observer, without a trace of flattery.

Macno bites his lips. He says, "It's not a question of being clear. Apart from the fact that I've just been telling you I'm not clear at all. The question is what we're going to do."

Dunnell takes off his eyeglasses, wipes them with a handkerchief, his left hand still gripping the seat hard.

"There's just a little over three weeks left," Macno says.

"Ottavio is re-editing everything with crowds from the archive, and the effect is grotesque. At this point there's no sense in taping my speech live; it might as well be done in the studio. I might as well let Ottavio have his way and let him make a montage of old speeches. He'd come up with a perfect job, I'm sure."

Dunnell puts his glasses on again, looks sideways at Macno. He says to him, "Why don't you let him do it, then?"

"How can you ask me such a thing, Henry?" Macno says.

"I'm not saying it to *you*," Dunnell says. "I mean, I believe it all depends on what you have to achieve with this speech. How important is this speech, Macno?"

"You know how important it is," Macno says. "You know that if my speeches on television hadn't worked so far we wouldn't have held on to control for more than a few months. You know how many sharks there are in the murky depths, their jaws open wide, ready to devour everything they find. Once the opinion of millions of viewers wavers, they'll rise to the surface and this country will be theirs again."

"I know," Dunnell says. "The point is: do you feel like going on, keeping this country on its feet, or do you want something else?"

"Why do you ask me?" Macno asks, alarmed, closing his eyes.

Dunnell says, "Because I don't believe this speech comes out the way it does only because you can't find the right inspiration. There must be deeper reasons, damn it."

The helicopter tilts, turns over the narrow streets of the center of the city, over the squares and the smaller domes, the little colored discs of the tables outside the cafés.

Macno says, "You're crazy, Henry. You're an absent-minded botanist and you don't have the slightest idea of what politics is. You think a man, by himself, can take on a whole country and then drop it, just like that? Why, I can't even manage to face the little decisions any more; every slight alternative causes me agony."

Dunnell looks at the roofs of the city; he says, "I don't think I'm the least bit crazy, but it's true that I haven't the slightest idea of what politics is."

The helicopter flies low: over a terrace framed by a laurel hedge, where three little girls raise their hands to their brows and look up.

THIRTEEN

That evening there is a dinner for Lanston, the visiting foreign minister. The stairways, the entrance, the corridors are under the surveillance of more guards than usual, more alert than usual, mixed with men from the ministry in dark suits, outside the doors of the great salon. The great salon is full of lights, occupied by real banquet tables instead of the usual little low tables set casually in front of the cushions. There is just a whisper of music from the speakers: drifting notes of strings, much softer than the sound of the voices. The waiters glide from one place to another, enter and exit like white shadows.

At the main table are seated Macno and Lanston, their wives, Uto Rumi, Lanston's chief assistants, his interpreter, Ottavio, ministers, members of the political part of the court, and some of the artistic component. Observed from a distance, the words incomprehensible, the scene appears stylized and unnatural, like a television staging of an official banquet: the smiles, the toasts, the little brief nods.

Lise and Ted are seated with Dunnell, Gloria Hedges, the Yugoslav acrobat, and people of Lanston's entourage at one of the secondary tables, set perpendicular to the main table. Almost all of them seem disappointed with their seats: shut up in self-reflecting conversations, snickering about familiar subjects. Every few seconds they measure with a glance their distance from Macno.

Macno makes an effort to involve his guests and bring them out into the open; he looks for points of contact, he speaks with full voice, gesticulates, thinks up matters to discuss, and presents them in the most interesting perspective, enlivens them with new observations. Lanston nods slowly, sips his consommé; his big head glistens in the light of the chandeliers, naked under his attempt to cover it by combing his scant hair across it. Every time Macno tries to approach him verbally, he withdraws into an expression of diplomatic formality, like a tortoise into his shell. He raises his glass; slow and sealed in his black suit, he is completely impervious to Macno's charm. His wife throws her head back from time to time, reveals her withered neck, adorned with a triple row of big pearls.

Lise and Ted eat without saying much, confine themselves to remarks on the food. The atmosphere is toilsome, so different from the alternation of distraction and attraction that dominates every gathering with Macno. The strain lies beneath the surface of the conversations, as the court's artists try to make their behavior more formal. Gloria Hedges allows herself to be served a baked filet; she says, "Beef. Obviously a really good impression must be made on the guests."

Lise eats fried squash flowers, looks in Macno's direction.

Macno persists in his attempts at communication: he describes something energetically, tries to transmit to his gestures and tones of voice the spirit of what he is describing. From time to time he turns to Ester, at a distance on his right, to ask her for a word that doesn't come to mind, but as if he wanted to seek an escape from the situation more than anything else. Ester answers him promptly, but always a half-second after Lanston's interpreter, who puts himself between Macno and the minister with simultaneous zeal. Lanston's head has become more shiny after the food and wine, but Macno's remarks, which stir all the rest of the table, inspire in him only the weakest kind of protocol assent. His expression is so slow and heavy that you can't say whether it comes from pure personal hostility or political distrust or banqueter's indifference. Uto Rumi steps in to fill the gaps of conversation the moment they occur, picks up the thread of conversation every time Macno seems on the verge of dropping it. Melissa is as stiff and formal as the guests; her faint smiles at Lanston's wife are returned.

Lise observes the scene, silent as it appears to her: fascinated by the pain that begins to transpire from Macno's every gesture.

Dunnell looks at Lise as she shifts her eyes back to her

plate. He says to her, "I believe there are few things in the world that Macno loathes more than a situation like this. You see how he's suffering at this moment."

Lise casts another glance at the main table: Macno's nervous hands on the white linen cloth.

Dunnell says, "Each time, he hopes he can establish a contact as if he were dealing with a *person* instead of the representative of a government."

The dinner proceeds toward its end. Ted eats two portions of macédoine of fruit; he turns constantly to talk with the ballerina from Milan seated at the next table. Gloria Hedges describes to Lise the countryside around the city as if she hadn't the slightest doubt that Lise has never visited it.

The dinner ends: Macno rises, Lanston rises; everyone rises and leaves the tables. The people stream into the adjoining room.

In the adjoining room waiters offer liqueurs and coffee, chocolates and almond-paste cookies in great silver bowls. From the loudspeakers come violins and cellos just a bit more substantial than in the dining room. The men of Lanston's entourage and Macno's politicians exchange professional observations, face one another, feet together, glasses in hand. The artist members of the court gather in stiff groups, careful not to mar the formality of the situation. Macno leads Lanston's wife to a window and points out to her different parts of the garden, brilliantly illuminated. Lanston pays some kind of diplomatic compliment to Melissa, who smiles at him, as distant as a queen. Uto Rumi and a couple of the minister's aides flank the women with expressions of agreement. The conversations entwine, without great variations of tone.

Gloria Hedges says to Ted, "You still haven't told me anything about what you did before coming here." She shifts her gaze around, in search of more interesting or more useful contacts.

"Professionally, you mean?" Ted says, with his demitasse in his hand.

Lise walks among the people in the hot light of the chandeliers, passes through a network of neatly composed talk. She grazes a wall, filled with boredom and uncertainties.

Macno touches her arm lightly; he says to her, "How are you?"

"Fine," she says, without the time to think of a tone.

Macno looks sideways. He says, "Let's get out of here. Please. This place is death."

Lise says "Yes," forces herself not to look at him directly. At the other end of the room Ottavio is turning; he smiles at someone.

Macno touches her arm again, says to her, "Leave after I do." He goes off, cuts through the crowd.

Lise waits until he has left, then follows him, on a wave of anxiety at the thought of losing him. She forces her way through the interwoven conversations, the slow movements that block her path. She reaches the door, goes out.

She passes beyond the palace guards and the security men and Lanston's men. Macno is at the end of the corridor, is turning the corner. Lise walks faster; the voices in the great room move off.

She turns the corner just in time to see Macno close a door. Here, too, there are guards, with earpieces and little submachine guns over their shoulder, but they stick to the walls, without expression. Lise reaches the door; she enters.

In the room, paneled with inlaid wood, Macno is laughing, one hand at the base of his neck. He comes to embrace Lise; he says to her "Hey!"

"Hey!" Lise says, swept away by euphoria. Suddenly it seems to her that she is very far away from all the rest, in an oasis of pure and childish sensations.

Macno says, "My God, we did it." He holds her a few centimeters away, looks at her with an amused light in his eyes. He says, "We escaped, damn it." He kisses her on the forehead, rumples her hair.

Lise presses her head against his shoulder, runs her hands over his back; she breathes in his smell, absorbs with the pads of her fingertips the substance of his jacket.

Macno holds her away again; he says, "Those formal, arrogant bastards. You saw how revolting they are? You saw what slow eyes he has, how he combs the little hair he has?"

Lise laughs; she says, "I saw how you were suffering, you poor thing. I don't know what I would have done to set you free."

"And his wife?" Macno says. "With that tortoise neck, all wrinkles, and that dim smile? Damn bastards, they think they can infect everybody with their behavior, like a bunch of mummies."

"I don't know what I would have done, really," Lise says to him, trying to hold him closer.

Macno looks into her eyes again, smiles, embraces her. He says, "I know, I know, my pretty. But we've escaped now and we never have to see them again."

They kiss and hold each other still harder, and now they really are very distant from all the rest.

Then Macno says, "Let's go somewhere else."

Lise looks at him, from very close, tries to filter into a clear thought the many confused thoughts that are whirling in her head. She says, "But won't there be a diplomatic incident if you disappear like this?"

"I don't think so," Macno says, puzzled for a moment. He says, "Uto will invent some excuse."

"But Lanston will be mortally insulted," Lise says. She doesn't clearly understand why she says it to him; she is terrified at the idea that he might suddenly turn rational and decide to go back to the drawing room.

"He will?" Macno says. He reaches out to stroke her ear. He says, "They wouldn't have granted us the loan in any case." He takes her hand, says, "Come."

They go to one of the walls of inlaid wood; Macno presses two points and a hidden door opens. They go through the door, into an almost dark little room. From his pocket Macno takes out a magnetic key, turns it in the lock of a second little door, of metal. He points out to Lise a descending circular staircase; he precedes her down the first steps, then turns to make sure she is following him closely.

At the bottom of the steps there is a little room exactly like the one above, and a second door. Macno unlocks it with his magnetic key; he gives Lise his hand, leads her inside, shuts the door.

They are in a large room with curved white walls, occupied by a curved pool, like a little natural pond. The floor is covered with coconut fiber, springy underfoot;

papyrus and ferns in planters turn the light green that rises from little spots.

Lise looks around; she says, "What is this place?"

"It's a place for water," Macno says. He presses a switch: the pool comes alight, bluish and quavering.

Lise says, "And nobody knows it's here?"

"You know now," Macno says. The air is warm, so thick that it muffles voices and steeps the void around movements, leaving no space for difficulty.

Lise laughs; she looks at the little apertures in the ceiling, through which shafts of nocturnal light enter.

Macno takes off his clothes, dropping them at random; he goes to the edge of the pool and dives in. He swims on the bottom, smooth and natural as a marine animal, from one end of the great pool to the other. He turns underwater, swims back; he surfaces at the feet of Lise, who has bent to look at him. He huffs, takes a deep breath; he says "Aaahhh." He slaps the water with the flat of one hand, produces a spray of miniscule, luminescent drops. He says "Come in."

Lise goes over to a potted papyrus; she kicks off her shoes, slips off the black suit, stockings, pants. She runs on tiptoe to the water, dives in.

The water is warm like the light, salty and thick. Lise takes a few strokes and returns slowly to the surface. Macno is not far away; he looks at her and submerges. Lise goes underwater again, swims toward the little lights on the bottom, which illuminate the bubbles released by the thousands at every movement. She kicks her feet to combat the density of the liquid, which tends to carry her upward; she allows herself to rise, turns over, making no effort to stay afloat.

Macno glides close to her, grazes her shoulder; he goes on. He comes back, creating spray and foam, comes to kiss her lips; he vanishes below the surface. Lise turns on one side and pursues him, striking with arms and legs; she allows herself to be overwhelmed by remote aquatic instincts that prompt new movements, sidelong darting, quick little slaps of her heels. They glide one after the other like a pair of otters: the length of the pool and back, following its undulate shape; side by side along the bottom, eyes open. They look at each other as they rise for air, puff and inhale. The ceiling and the round walls reflect their cries, the fragmented little laughter that reverberates, mingling with the splashing and spurting, the thuds and the dripping and the crystalline spray. The beams of the little spots bounce on the wrinkled surface, scatter the waves in millions of unstable points.

Lise and Macno glide close: smooth and solid, the same temperature as the water and the air and the light. They rub against each other, caress, and none of their movements is left to itself in space. The space is full; every movement carries a thousand others after it. Macno runs his hands along Lise's sides, the saddle of her back, the hard hemispheres of her behind; the briefest path of fingertips is distracted and made more intense by other and still other simultaneous paths. They slide one on the other, one inside the other. They allow themselves to be drawn together, closer and farther and closer until their thoughts lose all balance and their sensations melt and there is no longer any distinction between inside and outside, between when and how and where. They sink and rise, trembling always more slowly in the trembling liquid.

––––––––

Suspended on the salty surface, they let themselves sway, their eyes half closed and drops of water on their lashes. Macno says, "You realize?"

"Yes," Lise says, without knowing exactly what he means but thinking that she does realize.

Macno submerges, slowly returns to the surface, blows out water. He says, "You realize? How crushed we usually are by the force of gravity? How we contract to resist the pressure? The terrible *effort* we make to stand up and walk and lift objects, to play a role and persuade and seduce, to keep together the elements of a way of existing, the point of view and the angle and all the rest?" His voice reverberates, slowed and aquatic, but anxious, too.

Lise looks at him, and she seems to understand what he is saying independently of his words.

Macno says, "You realize the disgusting *stiff* life we have to lead usually, how everything constructed is made of hard and cold materials, of violent lines. From the moment we're born we're thrown among planes with sharp corners, without flexibility, we who are by nature so soft and elastic. Think what a city is, or a street, or a house. To escape we simply shift from the seat of a car to an easy chair to a bed. We can let ourselves go only there, in inert, confined spaces."

"And we're never close enough to the water," Lise says, her lips on the water's surface.

"No," Macno says. He shakes his head, lets himself float. He says, "In remote epochs there were water civilizations. There were tubs, pools, fountains in the cities and in the houses. Once even this city was full of waterplaces, and they went there to discuss politics, and to do other things."

"Then what?" Lise says. "Why did everything change like this?"

"Then Christianity came," Macno says. "The Christians had a horror of water. They had a horror of man's soft and elastic nature. So there have been centuries and centuries of dry and dirty rigidity. Religion kept people far from rivers and lakes and the sea; they couldn't use water any more, not even to wash." He looks up, says, "Just think. The dirty horror of the Middle Ages, the fifteenth century, the sixteenth century, the seventeenth century, the eighteenth century, and the nineteenth century, and this century until a few years ago."

Lise breathes, immersed in the warm liquid, alert to Macno's anxiety and his thoughts.

Macno says, "Think of what bathrooms are in people's houses even today. Stiff little rooms for performing corporal necessities and removing filth in haste. Think how they all try to wrest what pleasure they can from their tubs, narrow and short and shallow. How sometimes a pair of lovers slip into one together and try to stay there as long as possible, cramped between the sides, their knees raised, unable to move or to turn, looking at the cold tiles and the WC nearby. And outside there are floors and walls, furniture and stairs and sidewalks and streets, hard and without any flexibility. And violent noises and air that's difficult to breathe."

They are motionless in the water, absorbed by the faint hum of the lamps, by the slow dripping.

Lise moves to Macno, says to him, "But now we're here and we've escaped."

"Yes," Macno says, and they embrace again, with more anxiousness than before, and a desire to let themselves drift with the currents that rise from the distant depths of the brain and the stomach.

They come out of the water and go to dry off under a jet of hot air. The air seems much thinner than before; the space is already emptier. Macno kisses Lise's ear, bends to kiss a nipple. Lise smiles, leans backward.

They go to hunt for their scattered clothes, slip them on with random movements. Lise says, "I wonder what time it is," and her voice seems oddly shrill.

Macno looks at his watch; he says, "Four o'clock." He points to the ceiling, says, "They must have gone to bed long ago." It is obvious now that he is tired: his eyes are hollow.

"Are you tired?" Lise asks him. There is no distance between them, but the idea of speaking so familiarly to him seems strange.

Macno says, "No, why?" even if it's four o'clock, and his eyes are hollow and his voice is slightly hoarse and slow.

Lise says, "I could stay here all night." She holds him, rests her brow on his chest.

"One of these times we will," Macno says.

"Do you stay often?" Lise asks him.

"No," Macno says. He points to a blue door and says to her, "I'll show you the rest. Come."

They move through the other underground rooms, curved and circular like igloos. There is a gym, a music room, a reading room, its walls are covered with books. Macno points upward, to the little glass portholes from which the shadow of the night garden falls. He says, "You can't see it now, but there's an incredibly complicated system of mirrors. The light outlets are very far away—

nobody can know what they're for." He says this without real attention; his words and his gestures fall where he drops them.

Lise follows him, looking absently at what he points out to her, and it seems to her that this brief walk serves only to create a break of some kind between the water and the palace to which they must return. It seems to her that the distance between them started growing again the moment they came out of the pool and began to dry off, and grew and grew as they dressed and other thoughts were entering Macno's head. A thread of anxiety rises to streak the torpor that enfolds them.

And Macno says, "I'm afraid we have to go back up there."

They climb the circular staircase, come out in the room paneled in inlaid wood. Macno shuts the little door. They look into each other's eyes.

Lise says, "Good night."

Macno takes her in his arms, runs his hands over her still-damp hair: again very close for an instant. He says, "Good night, pretty."

Lise runs out before he moves away again; she doesn't turn to look at him. She walks down the silent corridor, where the guards are dozing, leaning against the walls.

FOURTEEN

At eight-ten, Ottavio is seated at a little table in the breakfast room. He finishes a glass of grapefruit juice; he looks at the time with a nervous flick of his wrist.

Lise comes in, breathless, goes straight to his table. She says, "I'm terribly sorry. I didn't hear the alarm." She has a notepad in her hand.

"Never mind," Ottavio says, standing to greet her: polite, but reserved. He says, "Will you have something?"

"No, no, thanks; I'm not hungry," Lise says. She has dressed in haste, a blue blouse and gray slacks; applied her makeup in haste, with careless strokes of pencil around the eyes. She bends to fasten a gray shoe.

Ottavio looks at the door; he says, "Well, in that case we can go."

Lise follows him along the corridors, toward the official part of the palace. She says, "I'm sorry to be so late."

"Don't worry," Ottavio says to her. "The only problem is that at nine-fifteen I have a meeting, and it's a shame to have too little time."

Lise says, "As a rule I'm punctual. But last night I didn't sleep well."

"Was there too much noise from the reception?" Ottavio asks, without looking at her, as they climb the stairs.

"A bit," Lise says. She walks rapidly, to keep up with him on the steps, down the corridor of the second floor.

Ottavio slips a magnetic key into a door, opens it.

They enter a little projection room, half filled with blue metal cabinets marked with numbers and code words in yellow letters. There is a video screen on one wall, four or five orange chairs. There is an odor of carpeting glue; the air conditioning is too cold.

Ottavio looks at his watch, says, "Listen. This is what we'll do: we'll take an overall look, to give you an idea, then we'll come back in the next few days and look more calmly. Nobody's rushing us, after all."

"Fine," Lise says. She sits in a chair. She is thirsty and hungry and has a slight headache; the air conditioning chills her stomach.

Ottavio looks at the metal cabinets; he says, "Now then. Where shall we start? Here you're in the inner sanctum of Macnology. There is *everything* Macno has done for television in nine years." His tone is different from what it was a few minutes ago, when he was walking up the steps, cold and efficient; there is an ironic glint in his eyes.

Lise says, "I don't know. Let's start at the beginning. With something interesting."

"From the beginning . . ." Ottavio says. He unlocks one of the cabinets, bends to read the spines of the cassettes, marked by symbols and color-coded. He says, "So, then. Ah, there's this. It's one of the very first things he did."

"Good," Lise says. "Let's see it."

Ottavio takes the cassette, slips it out of its case, sticks it into the video projector. He turns off the lights, comes and sits down beside Lise.

The screen glows with a white light; yellow, red. An iron cage appears, in which a jaguar paces back and forth with a nervous stride. The credits unfold, against a background of percussive music mixed with traffic sounds and animal cries. Lise watches intently, with a faint hint of nausea, her eyes smarting. The credits end, the camera shifts from the cage to a semi-garden space where mothers are dragging children along by the hand; to Macno, who looks into the camera, leaning against a lamppost, ready to speak. Lise gnaws her thumbnail. The quality of the photography isn't good, the colors are false, and yet she reacts at seeing Macno so young and different. She looks at him as he looks into the camera; she tries to bring his features back to the ones she knows so well. His hair is longer and thicker, the features of his face are less strong somehow, less cutting, attenuated in a face with softer, fuller lines. And his way of standing is different. His way of dressing: a jacket of green flannel and a plaid shirt, tight cotton slacks and gray jogging shoes. He's actually too plain and accessible, from today's point of view.

Ottavio turns to observe her reactions; he says, "It's a historic document, chiefly."

Lise doesn't answer; she continues staring at the screen with concentrated attention. Then Macno begins to speak and move, and his characteristics emerge, pass through the immature features and the ordinary clothes, through the false color and the poor audio and the ugly takes by the cameraman, who keeps moving forward and backward with the zoom and digressing with useless pans. His gaze comes out, and some gestures, some tones of voice. They remain distinct and recognizable for a few seconds; they are lost in expressions and gestures still not fixed; they re-emerge more clearly than before. Lise watches the young and unknown Macno walking along beside a cage of bear cats: for a moment he seems the same man she made love with in the water a few hours ago, and a moment later he seems only the distant link in the chain of an evolution. Apprehensively she takes in every little lapse of expression, every slight hesitation, every minor mistake in the choice of tempo. She tries to figure out if she would have been equally fascinated, meeting him still so imperfect and in search of himself. She watches him as he moves through the zoo, speaking, and she would like to be less intent.

Ottavio says, "Do you want to see it all, or shall we move on to something else?"

"Something else, perhaps," Lise says. She keeps staring at the screen during the time it takes Ottavio to reach the projector: Macno young and unknown turns and dissolves halfway through a word.

Ottavio removes the cassette, goes and puts it back in its place. He says, "It's no masterpiece, surely, but he's already himself, don't you think?"

"Yes," Lise says, with a hand on her stomach.

Ottavio runs his fingers over the spines of the video cassettes in a row; he says, "Now what would you like to see?"

"Something more recent," Lise says. She is beginning to feel very hungry, and the air conditioning is icy.

Ottavio takes out a cassette, says, "This is from six years ago." He sticks it into the projector, comes back and sits down.

On the screen a succession of cars and buses and trams appears, on a rainy day with scant light: wheels and windows and exhaust pipes, flashing indicators, bumpers, windshield wipers to and fro; darting and braking, traffic lights, clouds of gas. The soundtrack is an agitated crescendo; the cutting of the images follows its rhythm. Among the close shots of moving vehicles, faces and gestures surface, caught through the windows and along the sidewalks: hands slamming wheels, sidelong, desolate glances; coat collars turned up; frantic feet on the pavement, nervous looks, hands thrust into pockets, pulled out again.

Ottavio says, "He made this with such bitterness."

"Why bitterness?" Lise says, looking at the people with haggard faces, gliding past the shopwindows, running across the streets, collecting anxiously at the bus stops.

"Well, Macno has always so hated the idea of being

born and growing up in that city," Ottavio says. "He can hardly ever speak of it with detachment."

"Why?" Lise says. On the screen the broken-up movements of traffic and people are relentlessly patched together, driven by the obsessive beat of the music.

Ottavio turns to look at Lise in profile; he says, "Have you ever been there?"

"No," Lise says, staring at the screen.

Ottavio says, "It's a very ugly city, and sad. Even now, after everything Macno's done, it's one of the most polluted places in the world. The average inhabitant lives five years less than in any other part of the country. Macno says that it represents the horror of paleoindustrial civilization, in its essence."

Lise observes the city as it appears in brief long shots: the squares without trees and colors, the buildings with small windows, the dark streets flowing with rivers and rivers of traffic.

Ottavio says, "But the thing Macno refuses to admit is that he's the way he is because he grew up in a place like that. He surely wouldn't be what he is if he had grown up here, for example, or in any other, more pleasant city. If he hadn't started out with such a clear picture of how the world and life should *not* be."

The images on the screen run on, to the hammering cadence of the drums.

Ottavio says, "The most amusing thing is that the cost of the documentary was underwritten by the city authorities. You should have seen the face of the mayor and the commissioners at the preview. They had always been so pleased with themselves, running a modern and dynamic metropolis, and then Macno came out with this image of a wretched old factory of neuroses."

"You mean, he's not in it?" Lise asks, disappointed.

"No," Ottavio says. He smiles in the semidarkness; he says, "Now let's put something else on. That was just to show you a bit of everything."

"Of course," Lise says as he turns off the projector and turns on the lights.

Ottavio goes back to the blue metal cabinets. He says, "Shall we move on to *Collisions?*"

"Yes," Lise says. It occurs to her that last night is already far away, and is moving further still. She says, "Yes, *Collisions.*"

Ottavio runs his fingers over the spines of the cassettes, takes one out. He says, "This is the first, with Tarminelli." He glances rapidly at his watch, he says, "We have time to take a look at this, and then for today we have to stop, unfortunately."

"Let's look at the last, then," Lise says, her head turned, pulling one leg up onto the chair.

Ottavio hesitates, the cassette in his hand. He says, "But maybe it's better if we proceed in order. We can look at the others in the next few days."

"No, let's see the last one, please," Lise says.

Ottavio says, "All right." He takes out another cassette, puts it in the projector. He comes and sits down, clears his throat. He says, "Four and a half years ago. The last broadcast of *Collisions*, with Prime Minister Tuorli."

The theme music swells as the camera pans over the studio: the scaffoldings, the tangle of cables, banks of lights, technicians standing around, assistants pushing camera trolleys, with cameramen clinging to them; the set with the two armchairs, and in the armchairs Macno and Prime Minister Tuorli. The theme ends; the cameras move in to closeups.

Ottavio says in a low voice, "This was his biggest coup: to get Adamo Tuorli to come."

On the screen Macno smiles. He is wearing blue, conventional except for the collarless shirt and a little pin in the form of a kangaroo on his jacket. His features are today's, his characteristics fixed definitively; the youthful imperfection of the video at the zoo is already far away. He smiles into the camera and greets the viewers, and the intensity of his gaze and his movements passes through the camera without being dulled for a moment.

Lise follows every gesture carefully, collects the nuances of every word: captured as if she were following the broadcast live.

Macno makes a rapid introduction, summarizes the salient points of Tuorli's political activities. Tuorli confirms the words with a faint movement of his head, with its thick hair; he lights a cigarette. Macno asks him a generic question, expressed with great formal politeness. Tuorli waits a couple of seconds before answering, inhales smoke from his cigarette. The lights are reflected in his eyeglasses, but the eyes behind the glass seem distant when they are visible, lost in considerations and balances parallel to the words. The words come from his lips articulated and distant, as if in a declaration given as testimony; his accent is neutral in an unnatural way, constantly restrained from lapsing into regional cadences and slurring. He turns his head toward Macno, toward the camera, and it is clear he is speaking to neither of the two but is, rather, intent on a self-reflecting composition. His ample body is settled in the little studio chair; he speaks as if all those listening to him were ready to amplify his every gesture, his least allusion.

Ottavio says, "It's incredible to see them together. They're like animals of two different species."

"And they *are*," Lise says, observing them seated face to face: sure of themselves in such different ways, tensed in such different ways. Their bodies are different, their way of wearing clothes and sitting down, their voices, their glances.

Ottavio says, "I'll show you the interesting part"; he reaches for the projector, sends the images fast-forward: Macno and Tuorli move jerkily in their chairs.

"But it's all interesting," Lise says. "I want to see it all."

"I know," Ottavio says. "But we can't manage it to-day. We'll see the rest within the next few days." He presses a button; the images and voices turn normal again.

On the screen, Macno leans on the arm of his chair; he says, "Mr. Tuorli, there's one question that I imagine millions of viewers would like to ask you at this moment."

Tuorli nods cautiously, his eyes alert, reflecting simultaneous calculations.

Macno says, "How are you planning to resolve our involvement in Ecuador?"

Tuorli leans farther back in his chair, crosses his legs, lets his gaze run across the floor. He takes a breath, as if he were collecting from afar a great variety of thoughts not easy to express. He says, "Well, I'll give you a very clear answer."

132

Macno looks straight into his eyes, with no sign of friendliness or agreement.

Adamo Tuorli says, "As things stand at the present time we can't overlook the possibility that our position may prove to be less than totally justified in an overall picture whose lines do not appear to be completely established at this point as far as the other countries involved are concerned." He articulates every word slowly, without addressing either Macno or the camera; he barely glances at Macno when he has finished speaking, with a slight nervous contraction that wrinkles the skin of his cheeks.

Macno listens to the end, barely moves the arm with which he leans on the back of the chair, and behind his movements you can see his rising tension. He straightens up, says, "Excuse me, Mr. Tuorli, I thought I had asked you a very simple question, and you said you would give me a very clear answer, but your words don't have any meaning at all. You said absolutely nothing. You just strung some words together. Just sounds: do you realize that?"

Tuorli remains suspended; it takes him at least two seconds to grasp Macno's tone, his manner of addressing him. He takes another breath, shifts his heavy body in his black suit just a few inches in the chair. He says, "What? Hm? It seems to me that my position and the position of my government is clear as crystal. . . ."

"Listen," Macno interrupts him. "Do you realize that at this moment millions of people are listening to you in their homes, and these millions of people are not complete fools, and they listened to what you said the same as I did, and they realized that what you said was absolutely meaningless?"

Tuorli says, "How can you make such a statement? My government's entire effort in these past six months . . ." He speaks again, slow and distant, but in the cruel lights of the studio the skin of his sagging cheeks has turned red, so has his shiny forehead below the gray hedge of hair.

"Tuorli," Macno says. "Remember, at this moment you're not in Parliament, or addressing the members of your party, and you're not before an assembly of the vassals of your government, or talking to a yes-man from the state television. This is a free program, and the public watching you is free, and I may be mistaken but I don't believe they will put up with the systematic way you and your colleagues are trying to pull the wool over their eyes."

Adamo Tuorli seems for a moment to be looking for a balanced reaction, then suddenly he goes to pieces; his slow equilibrium collapses and he slips on the shards. He thrusts his chest forward, his face is red; he shouts, "I won't take this language! You are insulting me and the country's government! You want to stir up trouble; you're fomenting the worst kind of nihilism!"

"You're the fomenter, Tuorli!" Macno says. His voice now is so taut that it cuts through the shrill voice of Tuorli. He says, "Tuorli, people are sick to death of you and your friends. They're sick to death of giving you money and then seeing you throw it out of the window or stuff it into your pockets or hand it out to your henchmen. They're sick to death of the whole arrogant, rude bunch of you, sprawling like this in front of the TV cameras.

134

You and your friends are the ones who have brought this country to the brink of catastrophe, and I don't believe you will be able to act much longer as if nothing were happening."

Adamo Tuorli looks around, his eyes seeking the intervention of the director or somebody. His forehead, his short stubby nose are sweating in the glow of the spotlights. He says, "This is intolerable. I refuse to play your game. It is absolutely intolerable that a program whose purpose should be to—"

Macno says, "Tuorli, you are *never* sincere. You *never* say what you think."

Tuorli shifts in his chair, looks around, his eyes shining behind his glasses. His gestures betray the rising panic beneath the surface. He cries, "You're using a language that has nothing to do with the democratic methods of debate, with information—"

"I'm using a human language, Tuorli," Macno says. "You're the one who uses a frightful language, where not one word means what it should. You and your friends are terrible actors who treat this country as if it were a shabby little provincial stage. You are horrid animals who live off people and their activities like parasites. The only thing that interests you in life is surviving everybody and everything."

His face livid, Tuorli says, "I refuse to go on with this. This isn't journalism: it's gangsterism. The program is over! The program is over!" He wrenches himself from the chair, advances furious and distraught toward the camera, then off screen. The screen for another instant frames Macno seated alone; he turns gray, dotted with static sparks; yellow, milk-white.

Ottavio switches on the lights, turns toward Lise.

Lise says nothing, looks at the screen.

Ottavio takes the cassette from the projector, slips it into its box, goes to replace it in the metal cabinet.

Lise says, "I had read what the papers wrote then, and I've heard people talk about it time and again, but I never thought it was like that. I never thought it was that *strong*." Her voice is fragile.

"Well, it was the end of an era for this country," Ottavio says. "The end of an era, live."

FIFTEEN

In the afternoon Lise comes into a little room where Ted, with a glass of almond milk in his hand, is looking at a video of Otis Duckett. The usual people are there, chatting in armchairs, on sofas, with one eye on the screen and one on the door to see who's coming in, who's going by in the corridor. Lise sits down beside Ted, says to him, "How's everything?"

"Fine," Ted says, almost without turning, his eyes immediately going back to the video.

Lise pinches his arm; she says to him, "Are you still furious with me?"

"I'm not the least bit furious," Ted says. He stares at the screen with exaggerated attention: Duckett singing on water skis, pursued by a shark.

Lise says, "I talked with Ottavio yesterday, and he told me Macno wants to do the interview soon."

"He already said that two weeks ago, it seems to me," Ted says, his lips clenched.

"Yes, but this time it's absolutely certain," Lise says. "And he'll give us two hours instead of one, so there's room for a real interview, an important one. And, besides, Ottavio has authorized me to see the tapes in the archive."

Ted turns, says, "He has? When can we see them?"

"I've already seen them, this morning," Lise says. She reaches out to touch his shoulder.

Ted says, "That's perfect. Thanks a lot. You don't even let me in on things concerning the job any more."

"He only told me at the last moment," Lise says. "I didn't even know where to find you."

"Yeah, of course; *I'm* the one who keeps disappearing without a word to anyone, right?" Ted says. He takes a nervous sip of almond milk, he says, "*I'm* the one who can never be found these days."

Lise looks at his big reddish head and doesn't know if she's sorry or indifferent or irritated. She says, "Let's not fight again, please. If I'd been able, I would have told you to come along. I swear."

"All right," Ted says. "Anyway, try to set up this interview fast, because I'm sick of hanging around here. And I'm losing out on a lot of work back home. I feel like I'm in some kind of institution for enforced vacations."

Lise says, "You're fed up because you don't make the

least effort." She's mostly irritated now: by the stupid bitterness in his voice, the inert way he's sitting. She says to him, "There are lots of interesting people here, from all over the world, the most important writers and painters and directors of the moment. Can't you find anybody to talk to? It seems impossible."

Ted takes a brief look at the people occupying the chairs and sofas of the viewing room; he says, "This is a kind of half-ass little court. They're all full of jealousy and rivalry and hysteria: you can imagine if anyone has the slightest intention of talking with me."

"Why don't you try?" Lise says. "You don't try. You just sit there with that suspicious, grumpy look. Of course nobody comes after you."

"And what about you?" Ted says. "You're right in the swim, aren't you? Days and nights of giddy madness?"

Lise for a moment feels like revealing to him the thoughts she has in her head, the slow sensations that encircle her, telling him everything about Macno. But instead she says, "At least I don't go around complaining all the time. Damn it, we're in a situation that millions of people would envy, and this is how you take it."

Ted says, "Listen, everybody takes it as he pleases, okay?" He goes back to staring at the screen. Otis Duckett is finishing a dance on a jetty. Ted says, "You know very well that when we came here I was the most receptive person in the world, Liz."

Lise feels her heart weaken again; she says, "Then try to be receptive again. Let's try to get along and not fight, please."

"I can't be receptive again on command," Ted says, his resentment already cracking.

139

"Try, at least," Lise says. She touches his arm, leans over to give him a rapid kiss on the cheek.

Ted turns to look at her, he says, "You're going to drive me crazy, Liz."

Lise stands up. She says, "I'm going for a little stroll outside. I'll be back soon."

Ted hesitates between two expressions; he looks away. On the screen there is a video of the Rat Tats, dressed like doughboys in the First World War.

Lise walks pensively along the corridor; she goes out of one of the French windows, into the garden. The sun is hot, the air full of birdcalls and the buzzing of insects. She takes off her shoes, walks barefoot on the grass, trying to remember Macno's bare feet last night.

Near the lake, seated in the shade of a clump of elders, there is Dunnell, reading a book. He becomes aware of Lise only when she is very near; he raises his eyes, says, "Ah, hello, Lise."

Lise says hello. She sits behind him on the grass; she pulls in her legs, clasps her hands at her ankles. She looks at the lawn, the trees motionless in the heat. She says, "It's practically summer."

"I'll say it is," Dunnell says. He closes the book, sets it on the ground. He takes off his eyeglasses, blows on them, rubs them two or three times on the cloth of his slacks. There are bees in the air, and dragonflies and butterflies.

Lise says, "I saw some old tapes of Macno this morning." She doesn't really know why she tells him this; she doesn't stop and think why.

"Ah," Dunnell says. With his eyes he follows two

mandarin ducks that waddle to the lake, dive in, glide over the ruffled surface. He says, "And was it strange?"

"Yes," Lise says. She looks at her knees, moves them lightly. She says, "It was strange to see how he was at the beginning and how he's changed, how he became what he is now. I mean, you tend to think he's always been like this, you don't imagine the whole process."

"That's true," Dunnell says. He runs an absent hand over the grass, as if he were brushing crumbs from a tablecloth. He says, "But then Macno has never stopped changing. He's already so different from what he was when I met him three years ago."

"Different how?" Lise asks. Four or five different images of Macno come into her head: his ways of smiling, of moving his hands.

Dunnell says, "Well, he was much more *inside* situations, he *believed* much more in what he did. Now he has this sort of detachment, this way of looking at things from a few paces' distance, as if nothing were important. When I first knew him, *everything* was important for him. He was always so incredibly *present* and alert to the mechanisms, ready to dash from one place to another and overcome obstacles and arouse enthusiasm, stir up energies and inspire and overwhelm. Nobody could remain cold and detached with him, they couldn't hang onto their old convictions. Macno had such *strength*, such an immense supply of energy, he would have overwhelmed anybody."

Lise looks at him as he warms to his reflections, in his khaki-colored shirt, too heavy for the season. She says to him, "And why do you think he's changed?"

"I don't know," Dunnell says. He smooths the blades of grass with his hand, he says, "Macno is a complex person, and complex persons change. And, naturally, the general situation is very difficult—the enthusiasm and the fun of the beginning have worn off. This country was in such a disastrous condition that putting it back on its feet is an almost desperate undertaking, especially with the international isolation there is now. But that isn't all, because, in fact, Macno is stimulated by difficult situations, he certainly isn't frightened by a challenge."

"What is it, then?" Lise asks.

Dunnell looks at the sunny park, narrows his eyes. He says, "It must be a terrifying responsibility, having to act as guide and reference point, scapegoat and older brother to millions of people."

"But Macno has extraordinary gifts," Lise says, as if it were a matter of convincing him.

"That's the problem," Dunnell says. "Macno is too intelligent to be a dictator. He ought to have a thousand times fewer ideas, and a thousand times more manias, to last in his position. Macno is an artist, and an artist isn't an organizer, a convincer. There may be moments when he's able to strike a chord in everyone, and communicate in the most intense and direct way, but then there are others when he's so distant that nobody can follow him or read him. An artist is full of doubts, and in this role he can never have any. If you stop and think about it, politics is all based on the absence of doubts, or at least on a show of absence of doubts."

Lise is silent, looks at the fine, dusty leaves of a tamarisk, the glint of the sun on the lake.

Dunnell says, "And his position is also dangerous,

naturally. He knows that very well. Physically danger-ous, I mean."

"Dangerous, how?" Lise says, turning toward him.

"I don't know," Dunnell says. "True, there are all these security measures, guards and electronic gadgets. But you saw for yourself: it's not all that hard to get in, just climbing the wall."

"But they caught us right away," Lise says. "We only went a few meters."

"Of course," Dunnell says, with vague eyes. A hornet passes over his head, drawn by the elderberries. Dunnell says, "Maybe we always end up being overapprehensive when we know we can't do much in any case."

They are both quiet; they look at the motionless park, in the hot and lazy afternoon of early summer.

SIXTEEN

After dinner Lise is listening to Igor Trelic in one of the small recital rooms: the big bearded man with slim fingers is bent to draw a line of notes from the guitar. The listeners are motionless in the penumbra, settled in the little low-backed chairs. Ted is distant, enveloped in an exchange of looks and smiles with the ballerina from Milan. Lise continues looking around in search of signals; every time somebody enters or leaves, trying not to make noise, she turns toward the door. The music further concentrates the sweetish anxiety inside her, makes her breathe even more slowly.

Someone grazes her arm: a young maid with short hair. She smiles politely, whispers, "If you'll follow me I'll take you to where you're expected." She indicates the door with her eyes.

Lise is behind her through the room, out in the corridor, up some stairs, and along another corridor.

The maid walks lightly, two or three paces ahead, without turning or looking back. She slows down outside a door, points a hand at it, and walks on.

Inside there is Palmario, leaning against a wall with a book in his hand. He makes a polite little bow, goes and opens a second door, closes it behind Lise.

Lise steps into the room with the dim light. Macno is standing at the open window, looking out into the night. He turns a second after Lise has entered, says "Hi."

"Hi," Lise says to him at five meters' distance, uncertain whether to move closer, because he seems to her melancholy and distant. She goes to him, embraces him. "Hi," she says again, with half-closed eyes.

"Pretty," Macno says to her, stroking her shoulder.

She looks up at him through her lashes, still uncertain about his mood and his distance.

Macno looks out of the window; he says, "It's summer." A hot, fine wind moves through their hair, through the fine fabric of their shirts. The sky is clear, with few, very far-off stars. Macno takes Lise by the hand, leads her into an adjoining room furnished like a bedroom. He closes the door; he looks hard into her eyes. He says, "Thank God."

"Thank God what?" Lise asks, her voice just a shade thinner.

"Thank God you're here," Macno says. He embraces

her, and she goes to him with no thought in her head. They kiss deeply, almost without breathing: entrusted to a single sense.

They fall onto the bed; they roll to one side, compact and gasping. They rid themselves of their clothes, driven by a submarine eagerness. They glide skin against skin, they seek each other with impatient fingertips. They caress and hug and kiss and lick, and each sensation is lost in a gesture, each desire in an oblique movement, each tremor in close breathing, in a rapid beat of the heart. Lise tries to remain clearheaded, then lets herself go, sinks to the bottom of the stream, lets herself be caught up in a swaying that begins light, circumscribed, then spreads and spreads and spreads, drawing her back past the limit of balance, where she remains suspended for a moment illuminated by the clearest euphoria and then falls again through layers of descending sensations, into an abyss less and less profound, muffled and soft like the surface of the bed.

Breathing resumes from far away; she looks at Macno's sweating back, at the muscles beneath his skin. She stretches out a hand, lightly grazes his left arm. She says to him, "I saw you this morning."

"Saw me? What do you mean?" Macno says, turning his head slightly.

"I saw your old tapes," Lise says.

"Ah," he says. "Ottavio told me. But you shouldn't have. I'll have them all destroyed."

"Why?" Lise says, her lips just above the rumpled sheets.

"Because they make me sad," Macno says. "It infuriates me to have them there, filed away like valuable documents."

"But they *are* valuable," Lise says. "Think of me, for example. If I hadn't seen the tapes, how would I know what you were like before?"

Macno turns on his side, looks at her lips. He says, "What does it matter what I was like before? Does that somehow change what I'm like now? Or what I'll become in five years or ten?" He looks at his hand, moves the fingers. He says, "And besides—tapes, that claim to be much more and much better than an old photograph, so much more rich and complete and objective—what do they tell you about what came just before, or just after? Even a thousandth of a second after?"

Lise strokes his hand, says, "All right. Anyway, it was interesting. And in the first ones you were funny, with your hair longer and your face rounder."

"Rounder?" Macno says, raising his head. "What does that mean?" He puffs out his cheeks, expels the air.

"Idiot," Lise says; she laughs.

Macno slides closer to her, kisses the tip of her nose, her neck. They make love again: more clearheaded and slower now.

Lise gets up, goes into the bathroom. She looks at herself in the mirror, tries to figure out how much her face can have changed in the last five years. She tries to figure out how much it can have changed in the eighteen days since she arrived here. She washes in lukewarm water, dries herself with a white Turkish towel. She takes a bottle of aftershave from the shelf, unscrews the top, sniffs it: it isn't the smell of Macno, but it's close. She pours a few drops on her fingers, moistens her armpits, behind her ears. She looks at the circular tub, the towels on the racks and in the little cabinets, she checks herself again at the mirror, tries to figure out how much she might interest Macno, and why. She looks at herself in profile, strokes her right breast, follows the white curve with her hand, grazes the point of the nipple. She smiles at the mirror, leaves the room.

Macno is already dressed; he is tying a shoe. His clothes are completely different from the usual: sand-colored jacket and trousers of an old, conventional cut, blue shirt with pointed collar. He stands erect, raises his chin, says, "How do I look?"

Lise laughs: brief, shrill little laughter. She says, "You're different."

"I *have* to be different," he says. He goes and opens a closet. He says, "Come and see."

In the closet there is an array of jackets and suits in the most varied styles and fabrics, and every sort of shape. Macno opens two drawers, and there are wigs of different colors and lengths, mustaches and sideburns in little envelopes of transparent plastic.

Lise looks, surprised; she looks at Macno. She says, "What for?"

"For going out," he says, with amused eyes. "We're going outside." He rummages impatiently in the drawers, takes out a reddish mustache, slips it from its envelope, holds it under his nose. He says, "You like it?"

"Let me see," Lise says. She moves around him as he

looks at himself in the closet mirror. She says to him, "You're better without it."

Macno takes off the mustache; he says, "It itches, anyway. I've never managed to wear one, or the wigs, either." He opens another drawer, selects a pair of dark glasses from among many others with all sorts of frames; he slips them into his pocket. He looks at Lise, says to her, "Get dressed, then. Move."

Lise dresses hastily as Macno walks back and forth in the room. She says to him, "I'm all ready."

He takes her by the arm, draws her after him toward a closet. He opens it, slides a wooden panel to reveal a small metal door. He opens it with a magnetic key, enters, pulls Lise after him.

They are in a narrow elevator, going down. Macno looks at Lise with shining eyes. He kisses her on the hair; he says to her, "Will you tell me how I would get along without you? Hm?"

They come out into a little white room; Macno releases the lock of a second door, has Lise precede him. They are in darkness. Macno presses a button: a light comes on, and another and another and another, to illuminate a tunnel paneled with cork, its end invisible.

Lise says "Oh," looks at the neon lights that keep coming on farther and farther away, revealing a moving belt that begins to unroll with a light buzz.

Macno says to her, "Come," draws her onto the moving track. They allow themselves to be drawn along motionless for half a minute, looking each other in the face every so often. Then Lise takes a few steps, and Macno follows her; Lise starts to run. They chase each other, laughing between the corked walls: light and excited, their speed redoubled by the treadmill, with no sound but the buzz of the machinery and the soft sizzling of the neon lights.

At the end of the tunnel there is a little blue door in the white wall. They watch it come closer and closer; they step off the moving track. Macno opens the door with his key.

They are in a small room without furniture or windows, with two doors. Macno puts on the dark glasses, straightens his jacket. He says to Lise, "Are you ready?"

"Yes," Lise says, in an almost frightened voice.

"Let's go, then," Macno says. He opens one of the two doors, leads Lise across a garage where there is a short gray car; he opens a little door. He takes Lise by the arm and they are outside.

They are in a dark and narrow street, without sounds or traffic. There is a faintly vinaceous smell in the air—a distant odor of jasmine and garbage, gasoline and fried fish. Macno looks at the walls of the houses, the clear and dark sky. He says, "We're outside. We're outside."

"Yes," Lise says, leaning against his shoulder, to the pace of his stride.

Around the corner there is a slightly broader and brighter street with automobiles and motorcycles parked against the walls. From open windows come voices and lights, sounds of television. Two kids run by; a dog barks behind a door.

They walk along other bustling streets, where cars advance slowly and cats circle bags of garbage and couples talk or quarrel in low voices at the places where the shadows are deepest. They reach a boulevard lined with plane trees, traveled by waves of furious traffic. They wait at the curb, breathe the air sweetish with exhaust fumes; they cross, running. They walk on a bridge that spans the river, they look at the great sloping embankments of pale stone. Macno sniffs the air; he squeezes Lise's arm, looks at her constantly.

On the other side of the river they walk along an alley with uneven paving. Macno points up at a little lighted terrace; he says, "The first months I was in this city, that's where I lived."

"Alone?" Lise says, trying to imagine him before he adds other details.

"No," Macno says. "I was the guest of two bad actresses. They were completely inexpressive, both of them, so much so that they seemed sisters even though their features were very different. The only job they could find was dubbing foreign actresses more beautiful and more expressive than they were, and I believe this was gradually driving them crazy." He laughs, says, "We were in this tiny apartment with thin walls, dark and full of old furniture, and we were always so *tense*, all three of us."

They pass a little restaurant, spreading out with its tables into a square with dim lights. There is the clatter of cutlery, raised voices, and hoarse laughter; the smell of tomato sauce and roast kid. Lise says, "What made you decide to come to this city?"

"It just happened," Macno says. "After the faint stir caused by my first record had died, I thought it no longer made any sense to stay in the city where I was living. It was such a horrible place."

"I've seen it," Lise says. "In your video."

151

"Ah," Macno says. "Then it may seem to have a kind of grim vitality of its own, like an old, rickety car. But it's much more lifeless and loathsome than that. A young person could do nothing there."

"And here, on the contrary?" Lise asks. Two boys on a motorbike whiz past, leaving a wake of noise between close walls.

Macno says, "Here there were the movies and television. And politics, naturally. There was this tension, just beneath the slow, flabby surface. People were always on the phone, kept an eye on vernissages and first nights of movies and the theater and receptions and all the parties they could get themselves invited to. The two bad actresses I lived with had a telephone with a cord a hundred meters long; they pulled it after them into the bathroom and the kitchen, out on the terrace, in their terror of missing a single call. Every time it rang they hoped this time it might prove a turning point in their life."

"And you were tense, too?" Lise asks, smiling at him, tight at his side. It seems to her that she is gliding, not walking, through the shadowy little streets.

"Of course I was tense," Macno says. "Not the way they were, but basically it was the same thing. Everybody was tense in that city. Everybody was waiting for an opportunity, like everywhere else in the world, only in the rest of the world anyone waiting for an opportunity is convinced he has special gifts to display when the opportunity comes, and while he waits he works and works to develop them, constantly competing with limitations and models. In this city, on the contrary, they're all so cynical that the very idea of having special gifts is considered ridiculous. The only thing they're all really convinced of is that they have the same faults as everybody else, and that success is only a question of luck. So they're waiting for a stroke of luck, more than for an opportunity. The most they do is try to come into contact with someone who can hand out strokes of luck, the way you might allow the current to carry you close to a whirlpool and hope to be engulfed by it."

"But what sort of life did you live in those days?" Lise asks.

"I tried to work," Macno says, turning to look at a girl with dark glasses like his who is arguing with a group of friends outside the entrance to a beer hall. He says, "Television was just getting started then, but it was clear that anybody who wanted to make music had to come to terms with it. So I tried to interest somebody; I made a lot of phone calls, appointments; I went to meetings and discussions. There was a lot of talking in this city. And eating, all the time. Every time you wanted to discuss something, you had to invite, or get yourself invited to a restaurant; and talk and talk, sitting at the table for hours, between a dish of pasta and a glass of wine, a roast lamb and a fish fry and a dish of eggplant drowned in oil and a mousse and some profiteroles and a millefeuilles oozing butter and chocolate and powdered sugar. You arrived with a project very clear in your mind, the details simple and precise, and after a few courses your ideas began to blur, to stretch out in long, vague chains. You ate and talked and ate and you lost your plans along the way; points of view got mixed up. And in the end, when you

153

came out after coffee, you discovered that nothing had happened. That was when I began to run a lot." He smiles, looks at a big cat chasing another cat under a parked car. He says, "I used to go run in the park for hours on end, to forget the food and the millions of empty words and the disgust at living in this city, in this country that's old and little and slow and sick."

Lise looks very close at him, and she seems to see him growing sadder and more distant second by second. She is quiet, holds tight to him. They cross a street filled with violent traffic; they walk among dark buildings, in a stream of people on foot.

And at the end of the stream there is a square full of lights and sounds and movement. There are people seated at the tables of bars and restaurants, eating and drinking; people standing and looking at the columns of an ancient temple; people seated on the steps of a fountain; waiters with trays; boys and girls leaning on motorcycles; whole families of tourists with thick pale legs; couples very close; unshaven characters with kinky hair insulting one another and gesticulating near a wall. There are voices on many frequencies, clatter and shouts of restaurants, strumming guitar sounds; music from the radio in the hands of a boy with a low forehead and thick eyebrows.

Macno turns in every direction, looking at faces and gestures and ways of walking. He seems close now, and amused. He says to Lise, "Isn't it incredible? Well? There's this vitality, like an old amusement park. You forget, every time."

They walk slowly across the square, among the lights and movement. Macno stops every few paces, turns his head. He says, "Look at him," or "Did you see that?" He points: two stocky boys with cropped hair aiming glances and poses at three foreign girls sitting at a table.

Lise looks with him, to back him up, and soon she is caught by his spirit and she seems to be amazed by the less gaudy details, by the more ordinary attitudes and characters. She observes everything with the same appetite; she looks for details to be remarked, as he remarks them; she underlines them for him. They circulate in a fragmented way, drawn by the slightest gesture, by the simplest expression.

They walk out of the square, follow a stream of amblers into a street with lighted shopwindows behind protective grilles. Lise looks at the couples arm in arm, the herds of foreign girls, pushing one another, the men with glistening brilliantined hair, the heavily made-up women, naked beneath transparent blouses. She looks at Macno at her side, says to him, "Do you do this often, come out like this?"

"No," Macno says, turning his head this way and that.

"Why not?" Lise says. There is a sax player leaning against the wall, and he holds a single note beyond all credibility.

"Because I can't find anyone I enjoy doing it with," Macno says. He takes two or three bills from his pocket, drops them in the sax case.

Lise hesitates, says, "And you enjoy doing it with me?" She immediately regrets having asked him; she looks away.

Macno pulls her closer, says to her, "You know I do, pretty." But it isn't easy to understand how far away he is at this moment.

They turn into a side street, where people with cups or cones of ice cream are sitting on motorcycle seats or the curb and in cars and at metal tables on either side of the door of an ice-cream shop teeming with people, who enter and leave and dawdle. Macno says, "Shall we have an ice cream, too?"

Lise looks at him at from forty centimeters: so recognizable despite the dark glasses and the different clothes. She says to him in a low voice, "But isn't it dangerous?"

Macno says, "No, come on. Nobody imagines it. It never occurs to them." He smiles: really close now.

They pick their way past the people outside and just inside the shop, among the people packed and noisy around the cash desk. Macno says to the peroxide-blonde cashier, "Two big cones." He manages to change his voice completely, assumes an unrecognizable cadence and tone. The cashier taps the keys, tears the money from his hand, gives him the chit in the nastiest way: pressing it with her palm on the top of the cash. Macno says to Lise, "Wait for me there," points to a place at the edge of the most urgent crowd. He forces his way among the pressing boys and girls and middle-aged people with chits in their hands, pushing chest against back and shoving and elbowing and kicking to reach the ice-cream counter. He allows himself to be jostled by the people; he smiles at Lise, who is observing him from a distance. Then he opens a path to the counter, using his shoulders. He asks for the two cones, waits for them, looking around; he displays them to Lise from the distance, forces his way toward her, holding them up high.

They come out of the shop, move away from the people and the dense voices. Macno says, "Did you see how they were pushing, the savages?" He turns to look again; he says, "Did you see?"

Lise licks the plume of whipped cream crowning her cone; she says, "It's so sweet."

"Yes," Macno says. "It's all sugar, really. Pure poison, isn't it?" He goes on licking it all the same, and this also seems to amuse him.

They come out into an irregular square, in front of a large whitish palace with closed windows. People are scattered over the space in couples and little groups, strolling in the light of the streetlamps. There are tourist buses parked at the other end of the square; there is a dead fountain of gray stone. Lise and Macno walk with their ice cream, silent in the summer evening.

Lise turns to look at the whitish palace behind them; she says, "But wasn't that Parliament?"

"Yes," Macno says. He looks at a couple kissing beside a lamppost, he says, "In three years we still haven't managed to decide what to do with it." He sets a foot on the fountain; he sits down on the gray stone edge, motions to Lise to sit down beside him. They look at the former Parliament.

Lise sucks two fingers, sticky with ice cream, and wipes them on her skirt.

Macno says, "The first time I walked past it, I didn't exactly know what it was. There were two guards in green uniforms on either side of the entrance, and some people gawking in the square, chauffeurs and body guards leaning on the blue cars. Then the deputies began to come out, and I realized immediately they were members of Parliament."

Lise asks him, "How?"

Macno looks at his ice cream, sets it on the ground. He says, "They had these opaque faces, gray from living indoors in the smoke and the tension of their slow, repeated attempts to move toward the top, from the years and years of rivalries sometimes reconciled with great strain and then reactivated, from the years spent pretending to have convictions and feelings and passions and enthusiasms. They came out one at a time or in couples or trios, some arm in arm, or leaning on a secretary or a junior colleague, in their jackets tight at the shoulders and loose at the paunch, with their pants flopping over their moccasins with built-up heels, and they looked like bad actors at the end of a performance being repeated for the millionth time. You should have seen the way they talked to each other; and how they smiled, how they held a cigarette, checking the gawkers in the square with sidelong glances and posturing for them, holding themselves more erect for those few yards out in the open. And their signs to the chauffeurs waiting in the cars, their eagerness to be back indoors and safe, to run toward the usual restaurants and stuff themselves with pasta and heavy sauces and meat and wine and grappa, and to smoke more cigarettes and work out plans and establish alliances and prepare smart moves. It seemed so incredible that a country should put itself in the hands of people so clearly driven by the wrong motives."

Lise also sets her ice cream on the ground. She would like Macno to talk about anything else, closer to the two of them, and at the same time she wants to hear him go on in this animated way, with this passion running through his voice.

Macno says, "The strange thing is that this country has *never* believed in politicians. There have been periods of great collective pretense, but nobody has ever really been convinced that a government was doing something good. They've always known, all of them, that the politicians were false and dishonest, were only looking after their own interests; and were all the same, no matter what party. Everyone has always had this cynical, disenchanted attitude. A minister would be accused of taking bribes, or the mayor of belonging to the Mafia, and the people would say so what? What's new about that? Nobody has ever really been shocked."

"But were they *all* like that?" Lise says, looking around in the square.

"The ones who expressed themselves, at least," Macno says. "The ones who knew that their country had never been anything but a land to be looted for clans and guilds and little private armics devoted to abusing power and vendettas and threats and demands, sudden alliances and shifts of allegiance, changes of position and ideas, betrayals and ambushes of their own friends." He looks at the tip of his shoes; he says, "Then there was the immense pool of the unexpressed. The millions of people who never said anything specific, but didn't agree with any government or any of the alternatives that Fascists and Communists came out with at critical moments; and these people would simply have liked something else, but they didn't know exactly what." He stands up, holds out his hand to Lise. He says, "The millions of people unexpressed and sad and boring and honest, who live with families they don't like in houses they don't like in cities they don't like, doing jobs they don't like, without even succeeding in defining their own mental images."

Walking across the square to a street of night traffic and streams of pedestrians gliding along close to the protected shopwindows, Macno says, "The millions of victims of life, who at most express little marginal opinions and remain inert, watching time and everything go past, manipulated by others. With their dull and vague expectations, like ticket holders to a public mess hall. Never having any idea of what is happening, but always assuming that someone more knowledgeable has that idea for them." He seems so sad and distant now; carried away by negative reflections.

Lise says, "But when you appeared they came out; it was obvious that they were able to recognize what they wanted."

"Yes, but only after they had been prodded and shaken and convinced every time," Macno says. "After they had been persuaded every time and aroused and reassured and frightened and lured and flattered and shamed and seduced. And a second later they were already willing to let themselves be swept back by the current, submerged by doubts and uncertainties and fears." He turns to look at a police car that slowly cruises by. He says, "I don't feel like it any more. I don't feel like convincing anybody. I've had enough."

Lise forces herself to think of some reply, but she can't; she looks at Macno in profile, looks at the street. The double flow of people along the sidewalks is dwindling; the traffic proceeds in faster waves from signal to signal. Lise looks at a town clock that says ten after two; she says, "It's so late." But a little farther on there is another that says eight o'clock; another says eleven-fifteen.

Macno follows her gaze; he has a bitter smile, his hands in the pockets of his jacket. A bus goes by and makes the air vibrate with its diesel engine, makes the walls of the houses vibrate.

They come to the end of the street, into an immense square with separate rivers of traffic flowing together around a white temple with many columns. There is nobody on the sidewalks now; the cars and the taxis and the buses speed up in broad curves. Lise and Macno walk side by side in the night, which is becoming damp and noisy.

Then Macno stops and says. "Why don't we go back? We don't have to stay out here forever." And he has a fragile look suddenly: standing at the edge of the immense square, with his dark glasses and his sand-colored jacket.

"No, we don't have to," Lise says, pressing close to his side.

Macno hails a taxi speeding by; the taxi brakes, pulls over a little farther on. Macno and Lise get in, sink back on the seat. The driver moves off slowly, looking in the mirror as he waits for instructions.

Macno bends his head to one side, pulls Lise close, squeezes her arm. He says, "Stay close, Lise. Please, stay close."

Lise looks at him with apprehensive eyes, lips parted.

Macno says, "We are so absurdly fragile in the face of desolation. We're so *exposed*."

"Where to?" the driver says in a hoarse and suspicious voice, his eyes suspicious in the mirror.

Macno says, "Avenue X," not even disguising his voice.

The driver accelerates on the bumpy asphalt.

Lise and Macno embrace and are silent on the back

seat of the old car, which speeds in the night around the remains of old monuments flooded with white light, and fragments of altars and marble columns. Lise breathes slowly; and can't exactly understand if she is very sad or very happy, or very frightened.

SEVENTEEN

Lise wakes early; she goes down to run in the park, even though she doesn't much want to.

She runs along the usual route: against the sun on the lawn, through the citrus garden, around the lake, under the eucalypti and the acacias and the thick horse chestnuts, again in the open toward the palace. She does three laps without slowing down; a fourth, and the same images of Macno the night before keep passing over and over through her head. She tries to think of something else, to concentrate on the various shades of green; she runs faster, beneath the sun, already too hot.

She passes in front of the palace for the fourth time; she stops, walks, swinging her arms, trying to catch her breath. From the French windows Ted comes out, followed by the ballerina from Milan in t-shirt and shorts that bare her pale and muscular thighs. Lise says "Hey," goes toward them.

Ted says, "How's it going? Haven't seen you around for quite a while." He looks at her breasts through the sweat-soaked cotton. But apart from this he doesn't seem involved with her; he seems serene and solid, already in possession of another equilibrium. He turns to give the ballerina a sidelong glance, to check on her and make sure of her presence. The ballerina returns the same sort of glance; she shakes her legs to warm up the muscles. Ted points to her and says to Lise, "You know Margherita, don't you?"

"Yes, we've seen each other," the ballerina says, shaking her legs.

"Yes," Lise says, relieved at the idea of Ted's new equilibrium; and just slightly jealous.

They look at each other still: in motion, all three of them, Ted and Margherita warming up their muscles, Lise cooling hers. Ted says to Lise, "Zero news?"

"No, nothing for now," Lise says, looking at the sun striking the white stucco.

"Aha," Ted says, looking at Lise's left arm, looking at the ballerina, looking at the lawn. He isn't quite as equilibrated as he wants to seem, but almost. He says, "If anything new happens, maybe you'll let me know, right?"

"Of course," Lise says. She returns his wave, says, "See you." She watches him go toward the ballerina; they both trot off in the strong light, synchronized on the same rhythm.

She goes upstairs to take a shower, get dressed. She looks around for messages; she waits a few moments as she dries her hair. She comes down again and goes and sits in one of the little ground-floor rooms.

A few tables away, Gloria Hedges is seated, leaning on her elbow, talking to a little Indian, who nods. She turns every so often to size up the room with a glance; she sees Lise and rises at once, comes toward her. She says, "Lise! How are things?"

"Fine," Lise says in a low voice, without smiling or anything.

Gloria Hedges checks the people at the other tables; she says, "Mind if I sit here?" She sits down.

"No, no," Lise says, pushing her chair back.

Gloria Hedges fishes a barley cracker from a bowl, nibbles it. She looks Lise in the eyes, she says, "Well? What about the interview? How far have you got?"

"Far enough," Lise says.

"Ah, good," Gloria Hedges says. She turns her eyes away to observe a thin, dark-skinned couple on their way to sit down on the other side of the room. She turns back and again looks hard and close at Lise. She says, "I know how exasperating he can be, Macno. But it isn't arrogance or presumption, as some people might think. It's just that when somebody asks him for something he can never say no. I mean, if it's obvious that the person who asks is very anxious."

"But I didn't ask him for anything," Lise says, looking to one side. "I haven't asked him for anything, not after the first time, at least." She feels awkward now, and it seems to her that she's speaking English very badly, with a stiff and nervous German accent, one word against the next with no grace.

"I know, of course," Gloria Hedges says. "I'm only telling you this because by now I know him well, to the extent that anyone can know Macno; and I know how he behaves in these cases. He can't say no, not even when he is absolutely sure that he'll never do what he's being asked."

"And why not?" Lise says.

"Ah, that's hard to say," Gloria Hedges says. "He has some mechanisms that are so complex, and at times so simple. When he's trapped in a commitment he's always so surprised, he can't understand how he could have said yes without putting up the least resistance." She shifts a little vase of purple campanulas on the white cloth, she says, "I believe that every request seems to him to conceal possibilities or motives or ways of thinking that are worth being explored, even if only in words. He's always so intrigued by tiny details, so ready to let himself be fascinated by the slightest thing."

Lise looks at her lips, the round frames of her glasses, her carefully done hair. She takes a barley cracker, taps it on the rim of the bowl, she says, "Right," uncertain whether to stand up and leave or to find a witty, bitchy remark.

Gloria Hedges suddenly reaches out and touches Lise's elbow, and says, "Listen, Lise, doesn't it seem fundamentally absurd to you that the two of us are so hostile?"

"I'm not the least bit hostile," Lise says in a hostile

tone. She signals a no to the waitress coming over to ask her if she wants something.

"Of course you are," Gloria Hedges says. "And so am I. But it's ridiculous, and also a bit pathetic, I'm afraid." She adjusts her hair with a nervous gesture, turns to survey the room. She takes off her glasses, looks at Lise with eyes much less cold and aggressive than they seemed behind the lenses. She smiles, a sad and amused smile; she says, "Don't you agree? Why do we have to behave like two characters in a book of mine?"

Lise looks at her with surprise, smiles, says, "I don't know. I've never read any of your books."

"You're not missing much," Gloria Hedges says. She takes another barley cracker, crumbles it as she looks around. She says, "Christ. If we could at least allow ourselves the luxury of behaving like characters in one of Palmario's books, and always be so vague and open to destiny."

"What do you mean, Palmario's?" Lise asks.

Gloria Hedges smiles more frankly, revealing her very white teeth. She says, "Haven't you ever heard of *The Pale Aura* or *Unstable States*? That's him."

"Palmario. Palmario Gavin Llascas?" Lise says, dumbfounded. She stares at Gloria Hedges to see if she is teasing; she says, "Really?"

"Have you read his books?" Gloria Hedges says, with a lively glint in her eyes.

"No," Lise says. "I've heard about them but I haven't read them." She looks away, says, "I don't read much, to tell the truth. It's not laziness. It's just that books are so slow and tiring, as a rule. It seems I never have time,

167

even when I do. Every now and then I come across one that hooks me and maybe I can't put it down until I've finished it, and I go on reading all night. But that happens rarely. It almost never happens, actually."

"I know," Gloria Hedges says. "And we can also thank your wretched television. *Anything* is tiring compared with television. Anything at all. And writing has become such a marginal activity, so removed from the world, that only the slowest and saddest people still do it. The poor deskbound drudges, who are shut up in the house with their ugly wives, full of fears and manias, glued to their old typewriters. Anyone who has the slightest wish to move and to live in the world nowadays hurries to do something else. Maybe television. It's revolting, but at least it's not marginal."

"Well, you at least don't look like a drudge," Lise says. She laughs, says, "You seem hostile, but not a drudge."

"Yes, but I write garbage," Gloria Hedges says. She looks out the window; she says, "I remember the first time I spoke with Macno, I was so incredibly tense, I tried to make myself all beautiful and present myself at my maximum best, and I told him the titles of my books and he said, Oh, really, Gloria Hedges, the writer of garbage. He said it in the most polite tone, as if he were making a completely objective remark, with no implicit judgment. And he was intrigued by the idea of having a genuine writer of garbage in his court, naturally." She looks at her right hand, looks at Lise. She says, "In any case, Palmario is a real writer, and not a drudge, even if in his books he tries to seem one every now and then to please the critics."

Lise says, "I was so sure he was *real*. I mean, he has

the build and the eyes and the movements, everything."

"But he *is* real," Gloria Hedges says. "He's not the sort of writer who plays a role."

"Then how?" Lise asks.

"He was thinking of this novel," Gloria Hedges says. "I don't exactly know what it was, but anyway, the story is told from the point of view of a dictator's bodyguard. And since Macno has always admired Palmario's books enormously, in particular *Unstable States*, this idea came up: for him to be here and learn the details of the job. And now he's learned them so well that he's become the best, or at least the only one Macno really trusts."

"What about the book?" Lise asks.

"I believe he's thinking about it," Gloria Hedges says. "Even though when we talked about it last week he said that at this point he no longer knows if he wants to write a story or simply live it. I understand him: it's impossible to do both things at the same time."

Lise gathers some crumbs of barley cracker together on the tablecloth. She says, "How strange."

Gloria Hedges puts her violet-tinted glasses back on; she says, "Yes, but, after all, our own story isn't exactly normal. I came with the idea of staying a few hours, and I've now been here eight months. Macno has this power to attract, like a magnet, and then create a role for you that you can't give up afterward." She turns to watch a girl with long hair and wide hips leave the room. "And once you have your role, you're done for. It isn't Macno's fault, and that isn't why he does it, or at least not consciously, but you see how ready we all are to adapt ourselves to our little stereotype—the writer of garbage, the young journalist, pretty and naïve, the absent-minded botanist, the bodyguard who never speaks, and so on. Even if we're really different and don't correspond in the least to our image: that doesn't matter, because having a role is so comfortable, having well-defined boundaries to enter. It's more or less what happens in a family, or even in a couple. Except that here there is more room for each role, much more attention and more means." She takes off her glasses again, looks at them against the light. She says, "For Macno, too, it's the same thing, only his role is the point where everyone's hopes and tensions converge. And not only ours. Millions and millions of people. It's such a difficult role to play, I sometimes wonder how he manages."

Lise is silent for a few seconds, listens to the voices from the other tables. She says, "But, in your opinion, why should he do it, fitting everyone into a stereotype?"

"I told you: I don't believe he's aware of doing it," Gloria Hedges says. 'I don't know. He's always taken up with so many simultaneous thoughts, maybe he's reassured by the idea that everyone he deals with has his place, where he can be found at any moment." She looks at the white cloth, scratches it with one finger. She says, "But it's also true that when somebody sticks too closely to their role, without leaving any room for surprise, Macno is very quickly fed up. A person tries to meet his expectations, to enhance and maintain the qualities that impressed him in the first place, and when it succeeds, he loses interest. He moves off, for good. It's terrible. Three-quarters of the people that are here lost their interest for him long ago, and they stay only because he's too polite to get rid of them."

"But can't they realize that they don't interest him any more?" Lise says.

"Of course they realize," Gloria Hedges says. "It doesn't take much to catch on when Macno is no longer interested. He has this way of looking *past* you when he's talking to you, this politely disappointed manner. But nobody will give up. Nobody can take in the fact of being at the center of the world one day and on the outskirts of the universe the day after. They all try to stay as long as they can. It's terrible." She looks outside, she massages the base of her nose. She says, "And it's so hard to leave, my God. Normal life seems so lacking in equilibrium, slammed among a million poles of interest. Here there is this balance, this flow of energies in a single direction. Whatever is said or thought or done is in relation to Macno, in relation to what he says or thinks or does. You realize the difference only when you find yourself outside."

Lise looks at her in profile and seems to see her become fragile, puzzled. Lise looks outside, also not knowing what to say.

Gloria Hedges puts her glasses back on, recovers her composure in a second or two. She says, "Okay, now that we've had our little self-awareness session, I'll say good-bye; otherwise I'll end up not writing a line today, either." She gets up, holds out her hand.

Lise also gets up, follows her to the door. She says, "And how is your book on Macno coming along?"

"Lousy," Gloria Hedges says. She waves to a sharp-nosed girl passing in the corridor. She says, "I think I'm too involved to write it now, actually." She again holds out her hand to Lise, shakes hers. She says, "Anyway, I hope that at least we won't go on being hostile. Nobody wins here, in any case."

"No," Lise says, not sure what she means.

"We'll be seeing each other," Gloria Hedges says; she goes off along the corridor.

Lise remains in the doorway a few seconds, uncertain whether or not to go back inside. She goes up to her bedroom again, paces back and forth; and her anxiety continues to mount.

E I G H T E E N

Lise is sleeping, a superficial sleep, and there is a knock at the door. She gropes for the light switch without finding it, gets out of bed, stumbles over a table leg, crosses the dark room. She opens the door a crack: there is nobody in the corridor. But there is a little envelope on the floor of the room, revealed by the shaft of light that enters. She rapidly picks it up, opens it: the note says *Come to the place where we met on the night of water. M.*

Lise drops the note, runs to wash her face and give her cheeks a touch of color, put a touch of lipstick on her lips and blot it with a tissue, wet her wrists and behind her ears with a couple of drops of perfume, take a dress from the closet and slip it on and barely check herself in the mirror, pat her hair, put her shoes on, and run stumbling toward the door, down the corridor, down the stairs, disheveled, still fastening her belt.

There is no one around; the guards don't pay the slightest attention to her as they stamp past. From some door comes music, muffled voices, sounds of video games. Lise follows the corridors. She reaches the appointed door, opens it. Palmario is seated in an armchair, his head in his hands. He springs up, assumes his professional gaze in a fraction of a second, opens for Lise the communicating door, the little secret doors.

Lise goes down the spiral stairs, comes out in the anteroom with the round walls. Through the door comes the taped voice of Macno amid thunderous taped applause. He says, "But it isn't at all the way we thought." He goes back to the peak of the applause; he says, "But it isn't at all the way we thought." Lise opens the door.

Macno is sitting on the floor facing a screen: barefoot, in a short white tunic and white duck slacks. He turns toward Lise; he rapidly reaches out and switches off the video.

Lise comes forward, says "Hi," and now is no longer sure of anything.

Macno looks at her in silence, sitting cross-legged on the coconut-fiber matting. He seems much more distant than he was on the night they went out.

Lise stands and looks down at him, her cheeks burning and her head drained of thoughts. She comes close to him, bends to give him a kiss.

He continues looking at her as she draws back, with a suspended expression.

She points to the dead screen; she says in a faint voice, "If you want to go on, I can leave. We can see each other another time."

Macno says, "No, no." His features relax slightly. He says, "I don't feel the least bit like going on." He smiles almost imperceptibly, stands up; he says, "Let's go into the other room."

Lise follows him into the next room, its curved white walls lined with books.

Macno says, "They're so hateful, videotapes. They have that implacable, stupid memory, that inability to select the background elements. They can never be ambiguous, never omit anything, expand time or shrink it. They have only one time, which is time itself, and images that are the images. They show you only as much as they show you."

"But you're so extraordinary with television," Lise says.

"I hate it," Macno says. He looks at the floor, the big cushions scattered around; he says, "I've always hated it, two-dimensional and drab and arrogant as it is."

They are silent for at least a minute, in the hot light of the standard lamps and the ceiling lights, in the big rounded room.

Macno waves vaguely at the walls. He says, "Did I show you this place the other time?"

"Yes, before we went out," Lise says, her voice still unsteady. She looks at the spines of some books, tilts her head to read the titles.

Macno follows her gaze; he says, "I change them every

year, because old books make me too sad. When they're just a little bit old, I don't know, maybe five or seven years old, or even three, and even before the paper yellows, the jacket is already dated, the graphics, the typeface, the colors. Or when they're fifteen years old. Aren't they terrible?"

"Yes," Lise says, looking at the shiny bindings.

Macno says, "If they're *very* old it's different, because they take on an equilibrium of their own, in time, a nature of their own: they are old objects that are also books. They're not just ex-new, barely dropped out of the present." He turns to look at the books all around, lined up one next to another to form ranges of colors. He says, "In any case, soon nobody will print any more, and they'll all become old overnight."

Lise listens to him at a distance of a couple of meters, leaning against the circular shelves. There is a very muted sound of percussion, filtering from one of the other rooms.

Macno runs his fingertips over the spines of the books. He pulls out a thick volume, looks at the cover with distant curiosity. He sits on the floor next to a lamp, leafs through the book intently.

Lise approaches him; she sits at his side, adjusts two or three scattered cushions.

Macno slowly turns the pages, his eyes linger on landscapes painted in oil in the nineteenth century: the lakes and the hills, the crumbling towers, the oak forests that open into clearings where flocks are grazing. He stops at the image of an Alpine hut and two hunters returning. It is perhaps two or three in the afternoon; the deep, soft snow has pale-yellow glints. A little spaniel scratches with one paw at the rough wooden door, eager to enter. The two hunters are also eager to enter, tired and hungry in their thick woolen jackets, bending against the icy wind that stirs the boughs of the firs.

Macno says, "Do you feel a nostalgia for sensations sometimes? Nostalgia for a temperature or the feel of a fabric, or a smell in the air?"

"Yes," Lise says, and she realizes that all her nostalgias for sensations refer to the few hours she has spent with him or near him.

Macno looks again at the painting of the hut, devoid as it is of invention or genius, and so faithful to the conditions it reproduces. He says, "And sometimes I feel a nostalgia for sensations I've never experienced. Sometimes I only have to look at a painting or a photograph, and suddenly I would like to be in it and be someone else, with a past that would allow me to know all the subtleties of the painting and of what lies just beyond the frame, the density of the air and the spirit of the little objects, the tiny changes through which, in time, every single element of the landscape has passed."

"Yes, I understand what you mean," Lise says, feeling very stupid because of the way her voice translates the scattered and unstable thoughts that Macno's words inspire in her.

Macno nods, looks straight ahead. He says, "Every now and then I happen to wake up in the night and think of how many parallel possibilities were slipping away while I was asleep: how many millions of other activities in other places and other climates, with other rhythms and relationships and sounds and colors." He shuts the book, sends it sliding off. He looks at Lise; he says, "And sometimes I think how many women I would like to be with, each so different from the others."

Lise looks at him, her eyes half closed. She says, "But you've had so many."

"But not always, or for always," Macno says. "Not to the point of being able to share their slightest shift of mood, the reasons behind their every gesture, the layers beneath the layers of their ways of acting. Not to the point of knowing them as they were before I knew them."

Lise is sitting beside him with her legs crossed, and it seems to her that she is suspended in his breathing, absorbed by the nuances of his voice.

Macno says, "Years ago I happened to accompany the woman I was going with to a dress shop, and while she was looking for what she wanted, I started looking at the other women moving around among the shelves and racks, and in a few seconds I was filled with a terrible nostalgia for their ways of looking at a dress, their ways of imagining it on themselves. I felt a nostalgia for not having accompanied them along the street from home to the shop, for not having had breakfast with them in their kitchen and not knowing the light that came through their window, their reasons for being in that house, the sensations connected with each piece of their furniture, and the history of the furniture, the history of the wood from which the furniture was made. And I thought how many other shops there were in the same street, each with at least the same number of women looking for dresses, and how many other streets in the city, how many other cities in this country, and how many other countries in this world, how many different and unique sensations multiplied by millions and millions in the same second and scattered through space beyond any recall. And the sheer, dizzying impossibility of ever being even distantly adequate to this simultaneous infinity made my nostalgia turn into sheer anguish, as if I were standing over an abyss."

Lise listens to him, motionless; his words condense inside her the moment he has finished uttering them. She looks at his lips, his dark eyes. She looks at his bare feet, and she seems to feel her eyes cloud with tears.

Macno leans his head back, inhales deeply. He says, "One life isn't enough for anything. It's barely enough to give you a dim idea of what it could be, the way you can form an idea of a city while driving through it at a hundred kilometers per hour."

Lise gulps. The percussive music seeps in like an amplified heartbeat.

Macno looks at the round white ceiling, his hands on his knees.

Lise gets her breath; she says, "Still, compared with anyone else, you live much more." Her voice sounds slightly hoarse within the rounded walls; not at all convincing. She says, "You have a whole country before you, millions of people, and everything depends only on you."

"But that's not true," Macno says. "I also believed it at the beginning, but it's not at all like that." He looks at Lise, looks at her knees. He says, "Do you realize that I have to spend my time confirming data and maintaining relations and revising courses, running to one place to prevent a leak while leaks spring up somewhere else? And how precarious and unstable this equilibrium is, alternating between enthusiasm and disappointment, expectation and resentment, always on the point of tilting out of control and sending everything plunging the way it was before there was an equilibrium?" He stands up with a fluid movement, walks with swaying steps. He says, "And I don't give a damn about any of it now."

Lise follows him with a slow look; with her heart beating more slowly than the percussive music. She says to him, "And before?"

Macno looks at her from a distance, a hand on his hip. He says, "Before, but only at the beginning, and without having the slightest idea of how things worked, I thought that everything could change. I thought it was enough to *want* it, more or less, that it was enough to be sure of what was wrong, of the walls and the cages and the traps, the screens of time and the dams for feelings, the mistaken motives and the mistaken settings and the mistaken ways that make people's lives sad and rapid and devoid of pleasure. But even then I never thought I had a mission for others. Nobody who says he has a mission for others is ever sincere. Not even me, when I said it. I was interested only in my own life. Really." He takes a couple of steps, looks at the rows and rows of books. He says, "So I put together one by one the elements of the situation, and when the situation was complete and my life was there inside it like a tree in a landscape, I discovered it wasn't what I wanted." He has stopped at the other side of the room, barefoot and dressed in white cotton, like a lightweight wrestler.

Lise stands up; without thinking, she says to him, "Can't you stop, then?"

Macno looks into her eyes, surprised. "No, I can't," he says. "This isn't the kind of situation where you can just walk out like that. You stay, until things really go smash and the others get rid of you or wipe you out."

Lise goes close to him; she says, "Don't say that, please."

Macno looks hard at her. He says, "All right, I won't say it."

They stand in suspense a few centimeters apart: Lise concentrating on Macno's imperceptible breathing.

And when he extends a hand to touch her hair and says, "But we at least know each other fairly well, don't we," she slides to him with her eyes closed, as if she were hurtling through space, with no other wish or thought in the world except to be exactly where he is at this moment.

NINETEEN

In the sunny park the Yugoslav acrobat and a girl with her hair in a knot are playing shuttlecock: the two white forms on the almost yellow grass converge and part in little steps. Lise observes them through the panes of a door; she narrows her eyes and the light fades her thoughts, makes them still vaguer, expanded to pursue and pursue again the same sensations. She turns, and Ottavio is there with a cup of coffee in his hand.

"Hello," Ottavio says. He is bright, full of rapid energy; his day is barely a third of the way through.

"Hello," Lise says.

Ottavio says, "Listen. I'm trying to organize things for those other tapes, but you must be patient for a bit."

"Don't worry," Lise says to him. "There's no hurry."

Ottavio says, "The fact is, I'm so busy, now that Macno's away for ten days."

"Away?" Lise says.

"Yes," Ottavio says; he looks outside with blue, tense eyes. He looks at Lise; he says, "Anyway, as soon as I manage to find a scrap of time, I promise you we'll organize it. As soon as I have a moment."

Lise doesn't answer him; she looks at his right hand as he bends to set the cup down on a low glass table.

Ottavio assumes a more informal tone; he points outside, says, "Did you go running even with this heat? You are right to be so methodical. I never manage. The most I manage to do is a couple of laps in the pool at odd moments."

"But I'm not the least bit methodical," Lise says, almost without looking at him. "And today I didn't run at all. I just woke up." Now she looks at him as if he were responsible for the fact that Macno has gone away.

Ottavio laughs; he says, "Don't destroy a myth for me, please. Our beautiful German journalist with her extraordinary self-discipline."

"Oh, stop," Lise says, irritated and surprised by his tone, by the light in his eyes.

Ottavio looks at his watch, turns serious again. He says, "All right, I must go. We'll meet again soon, I hope."

"Yes," Lise says, drawing back before he can go through the motions of kissing her hand.

She goes up to her room, paces back and forth without knowing what to do. She tries to remember Macno's words last night, to discover if they somehow presaged his going away without telling her. She tries to retrace them from the beginning to the end two or three times, until they become confused with those of the night before and the night before that, with those of Gloria Hedges yesterday morning and with the glances of Ted, the glances of Ottavio, the glances of the guests who have lost Macno's interest. Her thoughts come to her in the light, then go back into shadow, then come out into the light again.

She turns on the television, switches channel channel channel channel channel; turns it off. She goes and looks out the window; she goes and looks in the clothes closet. She turns the television on again; turns it off again. She changes blouse and skirt; she puts the first ones back on. She goes down to the ground floor again.

She looks into the little rooms, where Macno's guests, seated on pale straw chairs, are savoring mint and lemon sherbets and chatting in low voices or listening to music or looking out the window. They move in slow motion; their eyes are without curiosity. They seem suspended in a marginal dimension, waiting for a signal to return to being or doing what made them interesting in Macno's eyes and justified his summoning them here and keeping them as guests at his court. They try not to waste energy in the meanwhile.

Lise walks in the corridor, where every now and then an assistant of Macno's slips off rapidly, heading for the official half of the palace with a file or a plastic box under his arm. The precision of his movements contrasts oddly with the vagueness of those of the guests who pass him, distracted as they are by the slightest details of decoration, bound to one another by threads of jealousy that unite them or keep them distant, depending.

Lise goes back to the glass door where she was standing when she encountered Ottavio; she steps out into the park. The light is dazzling, the air still. There are cicadas in the eucalyptus; they spread an insistent vibration through the space. Lise crosses the lawn, her eyes narrowed; she stops in the sparse shade of an acacia. She leans against the trunk and catches her breath. A hundred yards from her, two long-legged girls are stretched out in the sun, motionless in two white deck chairs. Near the citrus orchard a gardener in a straw hat is picking fruit from a tree and collecting it in a pale basket. The cicadas go on chirping and chirping on the same frequency; they make the stucco façade of the palace vibrate imperceptibly, every blade of grass on the lawn. Macno isn't there, and the day wears on without color, without any semblance of a rhythm or a reason.

T W E N T Y

The summer is growing hotter day after day. Lise borrows *Unstable States* from Dunnell and starts reading it in the shade of a pergola, in the motionless afternoon. And she is so dense and slowed down inside that she lets herself be caught up by the first description of feelings that she finds, lets herself be carried along with the story, not putting up the slightest resistance. All the same, her attention is precarious: distracted by a distant movement in the park, by the voice of one of the guests crowded around the swimming pool.

———

Ted says to Lise that while they're waiting for the interview they could at least film some footage of the palace. He says "at least," as if by now it were clear that the interview will never take place.

He films the park, the little rooms on the ground floor. He ventures into the corridors to film, until an officer of the security services asks him not to go any farther. He films closeups of the furniture in the little rooms, closeups of the windows, closeups of the guests seated or standing, intent on talking about themselves and about Macno.

Lise and Ted do an interview with Dunnell in the citrus garden. Dunnell speaks without even looking into the camera; he turns his back on the camera to look at a cedar four or five meters distant. He speaks without bothering much about the microphone, too: he stumbles over words, lowers his voice, breaks off halfway through a sentence. And he has no intention of repeating any of the things he said to Lise about Macno some days earlier. He speaks in dull, generic sentences, constantly raises one hand to his brow, to ward off the sun.

One night a troupe of young Japanese actors performs a drama of Shigechan Kaburagi in the park. From the trellis of fragile stakes that marks out the playing area hang strips of yellow and purple and orange silk stirred by the light breeze; the loudspeakers transmit cries of toucans and low notes of the synthesizer. There are taped crickets mingling with the real crickets all around in the park. The actors move in little jerks, strike frozen attitudes from which they free themselves with other little jerks; they articulate rapid strings of words with abstract vehemence. Melissa, seated in the first row of white chairs, stands up after less than an hour, goes back toward the palace: elegant and pale, followed by two or three eager people. The actors continue, showing no sign of being anywhere near the end, and to Lise, sitting in the next-to-last row, their commitment seems extraordinarily pointless, like a decanting of drops into the sea.

TWENTY-ONE

Lise is in her room looking at a video of Kim Howie and she hears a sound of blades striking the air over the palace. She runs to the window to look: the blue helicopter sliding obliquely toward the formal half of the park. She turns off the video, goes out into the corridor, comes back in, goes out again, runs down the stairs with her heart pounding.

In the entrance hall the guards are motionless in their places; from the French window you can see the helicopter standing on the lawn, two technicians in white coveralls checking it. Lise goes into the corridor, meets a couple with erect hair coming along arm in arm. She asks, "Has Macno come back, by any chance?" The two assume a surprised look; they shake their heads, and it isn't clear what they're thinking, or what language they speak. Lise walks on, she asks the same question of a maid pushing a trolley on which there are many little geraniums in blue porcelain pots. The maid, almost without stopping, says, "I don't know," as if she actually knew very well.

Lise goes out into the park; she comes back inside and looks in the little rooms, in the artists' workshops, in the flower cloister. Nobody knows anything, but the atmosphere is already different: gestures and glances are already much more focused.

From one room Ted comes out, the black camera bag over his shoulder. He says to her, "*Guten Tag, Fräulein Förster*," with the parody of a little bow.

"Hi," Lise says to him; she looks nervously at the end of the corridor.

Ted slaps his black bag, says, "I've shot everything they'd let me shoot. I've run out of ideas." He looks at the door he came out of; he says, "And there really isn't much here, after all. All the interesting stuff is on the other side, but there's no getting past."

"I have to go," Lise says, taking a step away from him.

"I'll come with you," Ted says.

They walk along the corridor, without looking at each other. There is the usual opening and closing of doors, the sounds and voices from beyond the wood.

Ted says, "Listen, Lise. I think we have to make a decision here. I don't know if you realize, but today makes thirty-four days since we arrived. One month and four days. And all we have is an interview with Ottavio Larici and nobody knows who he is, an interview with Dunnell that we can throw away right now, plus some interiors and a bit of the garden that look like anywhere else in the world."

Lise doesn't answer; she observes a guard talking in a low voice into a walkie-talkie.

Ted says, "Now, Lise, I agree with you that the life here isn't at all bad and it's not as boring as I said, but still we can't stay here indefinitely. At least I can't. It's one thing to waste a month, and another thing to screw up a career by waiting for an interview that's never going to happen. Let's consider it an interesting experience, and call it a day."

"What would you want to do then?" Lise asks him, looking at him just for an instant.

Ted says, "I told you. I'm speaking for myself, but I plan to wait for this Third Anniversary speech to see how it is, and then I'm catching the first plane to New York. You do what you like, but you'd be smart to think about it for a moment."

Lise doesn't answer. They turn the corner and there is Macno coming toward them, followed by Ester and Palmario.

Lise tries to hold off smiling at him, but her smile widens on its own, dissolves her features, exposes her sensations without filtering anything or keeping anything in shadow.

Macno comes forward, and his approach is incredibly slowed down: the last four steps take at least a full minute. Space and time expand, amplify every fraction of movement and hint of expression, and suddenly they contract as in a video sequence in which a few centimeters have been cut, and when Macno should be facing Lise he is already at her side. He makes a neutral sign of greeting, shifts his eyes impartially between her and Ted.

"Hello," Lise says, with a trace of smile still frozen on her lips.

Macno says "How's everything?" to both of them. Ester is behind him, sees nothing but him.

"Fine," Lise says.

"Great, thanks," Ted says. He touches the camera bag, says "We've shot a little footage in the meanwhile."

"Of course, you were quite right to," Macno says, as if he were speaking to a child. He looks at Lise, says, "Well? I'm happy to see you again." His tone is distant, totally devoid of warmth.

Lise remains poised over a sentence for a moment. She says, "Oh, thanks," in the most stupid of tones.

Macno looks at them both with his polite manner; he says, "I'm sorry, unfortunately I have to go. See you soon, I hope." He kisses Lise's hand as he might kiss the hand of an ambassador's wife, shakes Ted's, and goes off along the corridor, Ester and Palmario in his wake.

Ted and Lise walk on again without turning; without saying anything to each other or exchanging glances for at least twenty meters.

Ted says, "Shit. Did you hear him? You were quite right. Good kids. Thanks a lot. What about the interview? Doesn't he condescend even to remember the asshole interview? With that tone of his, the big generous host, as if we were two backward children, goddammit."

"Oh, stop it, Ted," Lise says, but in the tone of someone about to start crying.

Ted looks at her, surprised. He says to her, "Hey, don't take it like that, Liz." He touches her shoulder.

Lise draws back, she says, "Leave me alone."

"Okay, but don't take it like that," Ted says, trying to see her eyes, while she turns her head in the other direction. He says, "I mean, it makes me mad, too, but who gives a shit, after all. That's how it went. There's a whole world full of other famous and interesting people we can interview." He tries again to touch her arm, make her turn around.

"Stop it," Lise says. "Can't you ever understand anything, for Christ's sake?" An instant later she's sorry, when he has already drawn back, hurt and amazed. She says to him, "Excuse me, but you do exasperate me. . . ."

"If you're going to be hysterical you can go to hell," Ted says, red in the face. "I'm not your shrink after all, Jesus Christ." He strides off furiously toward the stairs, with the black bag over his shoulder.

"Wait a minute," Lise says to him weakly. She watches him go away; uncertainly she moves to a French window, opens it, steps out into the park.

The evening is fading, the air becoming damp. The automatic sprinklers slash spurts of water in broad circles on the lawn. Lise keeps out of their range, but all the same a few tiny drops reach her face. She makes an effort to think of anything that isn't Macno, and she doesn't succeed.

She stops at a lemon-verbena bush, takes a little leaf, rubs it between her fingers. The subtle scent revives her

193

sadness, deep and bitter to the point of being almost pleasant. She sniffs the leaf and savors these sensations; she looks at the distant form of a man running, insignificant compared to the great horse chestnuts with their dark crowns.

TWENTY-TWO

Macno comes up the steps two at a time, with Palmario a meter behind him. He walks rapidly along the third-floor corridor, stops at a door. The guards step aside; Macno knocks, enters.

He comes alone into the vast room, rich with mirrors that reflect the last light of the sunset. He looks at the furniture of ancient wood, the yellow daisies in glass vases on the tables.

He looks into the adjoining room. A girl, short and thin, is pulling clothes from a closet. Macno watches her free them from the hangers, lay them carefully on a bed, fold them and arrange them in a large stiff suitcase. Her movements are sure and measured, perfectly silent.

Macno enters; the girl freezes, her hands on a blouse just folded. Melissa is near the window, dressed in dark green; she turns in a slow movement.

Macno stops three meters from her, looks hard at her, without saying anything.

The girl leaves the blouse, slips out of the room.

Macno looks at the suitcase open on the bed, the other suitcases already closed, on the floor. He looks at Melissa, her long white neck; he says to her, "Then you're really going?" In his voice there is a distant and embittered amazement; and in his eyes.

"When I've finished packing," Melissa says. She has a measured voice, not rich in color.

Macno looks out the window; Melissa goes toward the bed.

Macno says, "I thought you would stay for the speech." His tone is not meant to persuade her to stay; it is simply a tone of statement.

"It's too hot by now," Melissa says. "You know how that irritates me. It gets so damp, and there's no escape." With nervous fingers she settles the blouse in the suitcase.

Macno looks at her, motionless; he moves close to her. He says, "Why are we so distant, Melissa? How did it happen?"

Melissa moves away; she says, "Perhaps you know."

"No, I don't know," Macno says.

They stand looking obliquely at each other in the center of the room: he dark and strong, she slim, with lines like a difficult gazelle. They breathe slowly, conditioned by the presence, so close, of suitcases still open and already shut.

Macno goes back toward the window. He puts one hand on his stomach, removes it immediately.

"What's wrong?" Melissa says, her delicate nostrils dilated.

"Nothing," Macno says.

"That's not true," Melissa says. She observes him from a distance; she says, "Have you had an examination?"

"No, but I'm fine," Macno says. He looks out the window, into the evening.

Melissa picks up a silk dress from the bed, folds it absently; she spreads it out and starts over again.

Macno says, "I'm fed up, Melissa. I'm thirty-three and I don't have any desire to remain trapped forever in this life. It doesn't interest me any more."

Melissa looks at him, the silk dress in her hands. She says, "But don't you realize what you did to have it, this life?" She hesitates, lips parted, as if she were seeking other words, more expressive.

"Yes, and it doesn't interest me any more," Macno says at the window.

"You should have thought of that before," Melissa says.

"Why?" Macno says.

"Because now you have responsibilities," Melissa says in a tense voice. "Because there's a whole country dependent on you. You can't think as if you were by yourself."

"But I *am* by myself, damn it," Macno says. "And the country no longer has the slightest intention of depending on me, in any case."

"Naturally," Melissa says, dropping the dress into the suitcase. "If you're a million kilometers away from any-

197

one who's listening to you, naturally nobody manages to follow you."

Macno walks along the wall; he says, "I don't want to make anyone follow me. I don't want to be responsible for anyone else. It's enough for me to be responsible for myself."

Melissa goes to the open closet, takes out two or three dresses at random, flings them on the bed.

Macno looks at the ceiling, at the objects in the room; he says, "This isn't what I wanted, Melissa. I made a mistake."

Melissa stares for a moment into his eyes; she says, "Would you mind saying what you do want, then? What do you need to stop being driven constantly to want something you don't have? Would you tell me *what* you want?" Her voice trembles; her hands tremble slightly. She frees a dress from its hanger, lets it slide through her fingers.

Macno says, "I don't know." He looks around; he says, "If I knew, I'd have it."

Melissa laughs briefly, nervously, a puff of air. She says, "Christ, Macno. When are you going to decide to grow up?"

"I'm afraid it's too late," Macno says with a bitter little smile.

They are motionless and silent for a moment; then Macno comes over and embraces her, kisses her on the cheeks. He says to her, "Have a good trip."

"Thanks, I'll try to," she says. She moves away, says, "I have to finish packing."

Macno goes toward the door. He turns before leaving, waves briefly.

"Maybe you're right," Melissa says to him.

"About what?" Macno says, looking back into the room.

"That it's too late," Melissa says. She smiles at him: the curve of her lips, every line of her face so familiar before he is outside again.

TWENTY-THREE

Lise is coming into the breakfast room and she runs into Ottavio, who is going out.

"If you like, I have half an hour free this afternoon," he says to her. "It's not much, but we can look at a tape or two."

"Thanks, but it doesn't matter. There's no hurry," Lise says, forcing herself not to let anything slip through her gaze or her voice.

Ottavio says, "It's not a problem, I assure you. I'm glad to do it." He looks at his watch, says, "We'll meet here at two-thirty." He kisses her hand, goes off before she can say anything in reply.

At two-thirty-five they are in the little projection room: Lise seated in a chair, Ottavio bending down at one of the cabinets of tapes. Lise looks at the opaque screen and gnaws her lips. She would like to be thousands of kilometers from here; or to be here but as another person. With her nails she scratches the arm of the little chair.

Ottavio says, "I thought I would show you something from the golden age. A couple of years ago. All right?"

"Yes," Lise says, without turning around.

Ottavio slips the tape into the projector, turns off the light, and comes and sits down. In a low voice he says, "Two years ago minus one week. The First Anniversary speech."

On the screen a huge crowd appears, gathered at night in a square of the city. The façades of the old buildings that frame it are illuminated by spotlights; shafts of white light pass over the many heads close together, the many bodies that vibrate, one next to another. The camera pans over the square: the other thousands of people waiting; the large raised platform. On the platform there is a man who comes to the microphone as the background noise rises; and it is Uto Rumi, slightly younger and thinner than he is now. He says, "Fellow citizens. On the First Anniversary of this new state of ours . . ." He stops, as if he were out of breath or as if his own voice were frightening him, amplified so disproportionately, spilled onto the square by gigantic loudspeakers. He breathes silently for two or three seconds; he makes a broad gesture to his right, shouts into the microphone, "MACNO!" He withdraws immediately, swept away by the wave that echoes his cry, the wave of applause and yells and gestures that swells the nighttime square. And on the platform Macno arrives as if at a run: a little, agile form, seen from the end of the square. The beam of the spotlights follows him as he goes to the microphone and detaches it from its stand, pulls the cable to himself with his left hand. He holds the microphone to his lips. With a strong gesture he shouts, "Welcome to the second year!" And the square explodes: the thousands of sensations and unexpressed desires suddenly escape the control of the individuals to whom they belong, merge into a single deflagration that invades the screen with frenzied movements and sounds and cries and simultaneous expressions. Macno stands before the explosion like a sailor on the deck of a ship: slightly bent into the wind. He waits till the sounds and movements die down, smiling slightly. Then he begins to speak. He walks back and forth as he speaks, turns toward one part or another of the great teeming square. His voice is taut, without apparent limits of strength or color. He speaks in short, simple sentences; he raises and lowers the tone; he chops out the words in cadenced successions; he stretches them, leaves them suspended, lets their meaning emerge with a moment's delay. The contact is continuous; there isn't one nuance that slips away not taken in. The collective attention is entirely united, concentrated on the lightest of his shifts of tone. Macno walks and speaks, his every gesture and word so amplified that they no longer have any boundaries, and a moment later his figure, seen in a long shot before the teeming of the square in the night, seems sustained by a totally transitory equilibrium. And it is the temporary quality of this equilibrium that multiplies and multiplies the tension that is concentrated on him. His every word seems to be charged with apprehension for what is to follow, as if the perfection of what he says would seem to refute the possibility of a sequence a few seconds longer. The thousands of people are in suspense, listening to Macno as if they were watching a tightrope walker on a very high wire doomed to snap. Every instant that the wire doesn't snap, the emotion increases, stirs conditions that no one has sensed for such a long time and never so clearly. Macno paces back and forth on the platform, and the meaning of his speech lies not in what he says but in what he arouses, in the uncontrollable fluxes and refluxes of energy, in the deep play of opacity and clarity and opacity that makes the thousands of men and women gathered in the square hold their breath, and suddenly makes Lise cry, seated in the little chair in the darkness of the room on the second floor of the palace.

Ottavio turns to her, looks at her in the weak flicker of the screen. He says, "What is it?"

"Nothing," Lise says, biting her lip.

Ottavio says, "Lise. Is something wrong?"

Lise tries again to control herself; she presses one hand on the chair.

Ottavio stands up and turns off the projector, turns on the light: Lise sobbing, bent forward, tears trickling down her cheeks. He moves toward her cautiously, crouches at her side. He says, "What is it, Lise? What's happened?"

"Nothing," Lise says in a broken voice, unable to stop.

Ottavio touches her wrist with very light fingers; he says, "Don't. Come, now."

Lise dries her tears with the palm of her hand; sniffs, clenches her lips.

"No, please," Ottavio says. He strokes her hair. He says, "Please, Lise."

Lise says, "I don't know what it is. Excuse me."

"You mustn't apologize for anything," Ottavio says. He takes a linen handkerchief from his pocket, hands it to her.

Lise dries her tears with the handkerchief and blows her nose. Sniffs. She says, "Oof." She makes an attempt to smile, it cracks at once.

Ottavio says, "I'm sorry. Poor thing. Now you make me feel terribly guilty. I never imagined it would have this effect on you. I was stupid."

"No, no," Lise says. She wipes the corners of her eyes with the crumpled handkerchief, dries her nose. She says, "What have you got to do with it? I feel like such a fool."

"Oh, stop, please!" Ottavio says. He takes her left hand in both of his hands, and strokes it with the greatest attention.

"I don't know what it was," Lise says. "I'm so ashamed of myself."

"You mustn't be," Ottavio says. "You mustn't be ashamed of anything. You have no reason to be ashamed. It's happened to a lot of people: crying at a speech of Macno's. It was one of the reactions he caused. And nobody was ever ashamed."

"But that's not it," Lise says, looking down. She sniffs, withdraws her hand from Ottavio's hands, rises. She says, "Well, anyway, excuse me for this incident."

"Please, stop excusing yourself," Ottavio says, following her toward the door.

Lise says, "Where can I wash my face? I don't want people to see me like this."

Ottavio says, "This way," leads her along the corridor to the door of a bathroom. He waits, nervous, walking back and forth. The air is at least ten degrees hotter than in the projection room.

Lise comes out again: with no trace of makeup now, her eyes just a bit reddened. She says, "Can you see anything?"

"Absolutely not," Ottavio says, absorbed in his gaze.

They walk slowly along the corridor. Lise says, "Maybe it's because of this heat that my nerves are so weak."

"Your nerves aren't the least bit weak," Ottavio says in a calm voice. He adjusts his steps to hers; as if he were accompanying a convalescent. He says, "But it is hot, of course, no doubt about that. It's fairly absurd to have air conditioning in the video library to keep the tapes from deteriorating, whereas we are free to deteriorate as much as we like." He smiles, but Lise isn't looking at him.

They reach the stairs; Lise hands Ottavio his handkerchief.

Ottavio says, "Keep it. You can give it back to me some other time." He grazes her hand, says, "And I'll come downstairs with you. I certainly can't let you go off like this." Two men go by with folders under their arms; they greet him.

"But you must have all sorts of things to do," Lise says, looking at the steps.

"They'll just have to wait," Ottavio says. "I already feel so guilty."

"What do you have to do with it?" Lise says, starting down the steps. "It's not your fault, after all. It's me. I don't know what happened to me. It's not as if I usually cry so easily."

"Don't think about it any more," Ottavio says, patient and close.

TWENTY-FOUR

Ottavio is driving rapidly in the night; he swings the big car into the fast lane of the superhighway that circles the city. He points out the lights of the outlying districts that flow past; he asks Lise, "Have you been in this country long?"

"Two and a half months," Lise says. She looks at his manicured hands in firm control of the wheel; she sniffs the subtle bergamot perfume. She says, "I don't know it very well, actually. I came with the idea of the interview with Macno, and I haven't had much time to go around."

"Of course," Ottavio says. He drives in an aggressive

207

way: pulling up to the other cars and flashing his bright headlights until they move aside. He says, "You were so brave, to pick up and decide to get all the way to Macno, at any price. I don't know how many of your colleagues would have done it."

"Maybe we were just a bit irresponsible, more than anything else," Lise says, embarrassed.

"No," Ottavio says. "In journalism a person should always take risks, venture anything in order to get to the information that interests him."

The car comes off the superhighway, slows down along the curve of an exit ramp. Ottavio stares straight ahead; he says, "In this country there isn't a single journalist like you. And those who say it's Macno's fault just make me laugh. There weren't any before, either; there never have been. And if you think about it, it's incredible, because for them this could have been paradise. I mean, with all the corruption and the plotting just beneath the surface, it would have been possible to come up with a scandal every day."

The car accelerates, speeds along the street that winds up toward the hills. Ottavio says, "And instead, nothing doing. Here journalists have always been poor employees with frustrated literary ambitions. They write out their themes neatly, add a little lyrical description, a pinch of populist rhetoric, a touch of envious moralism. They didn't have any wish to run risks or take personal initiatives. For that matter, this whole country was structured in such a way that nobody would take personal initiatives, or do anything particularly well. The corporations simply tried to standardize everything at the lowest level. Mediocre journalists made sure that there wasn't anyone better than themselves who might stand out. When a hint of scandal emerged it was only because the journalist had received instructions from his party. But even then nothing was revealed completely. It was a play of veiled references and warnings, like a game of chess. There was the same kind of stylization, moves within the squares, one move per player."

Lise is silent, she looks at the lights of the little suburban houses facing the street, the dips and dark waves of the hills as the car climbs swiftly, curve after curve.

Ottavio points outside, says, "Up here is one of the few places where you can breathe in the summer. And it's also enjoyable to get out of the palace, for once." He looks at Lise, says to her, "Don't you think?"

"Yes," she says in an unconvinced tone.

The car follows a last, ascending curve; brakes, turns right into a little gravel drive; stops among other large cars in a garden of ilexes at night, beside a building of stone and brick. A parking attendant comes to open the doors; Lise gets out, sniffs the light air of the hills. Ottavio comes to her side, points to the sky full of stars, the lights of the city in the distance. He says, "Not bad, eh?"

"No," Lise says.

They circle the restaurant. Ottavio stops at a side entrance. Through the glass door they see a scullery where waiters in green jackets go by with trays and orders in their hand, checked by a short man with a square head who gesticulates and gives instructions. Ottavio opens the door; the character turns, starts the moment he recognizes him. He comes toward Ottavio with a display of servile cordiality; he says, "Excellency, what an honor!" He bows to Lise, says, "Madame."

Ottavio slaps him on the shoulder, as you might pet a dog; he says, "Toni, we'd like to be quiet."

"Why, Your Excellency, how else do you think you would be here?" Toni says, leading the way as waiters smile and bow without restraint. He slinks along a wall, beyond a half-closed door through which many people can be glimpsed seated, eating and smoking in the hot light. He leads them into a little room with a single table beside a large window that opens onto the hills; he pulls out a chair for Lise. He says, "Here you'll be very quiet, Excellency. Nobody in the world will disturb you, I give you my word." He puts a hand over his heart, and there is a hint of complicity just beneath the surface of his servility: an indifference as cynical and self-confident as his squat body.

Ottavio says "very well" to him in a cold voice. He asks Lise, "What will you have?"

"I don't know," she says, looking at a boar's head and a stag's hanging on either side of a wall lamp.

"I'll bring the menu at once," Toni says with a bow that seems like an actor's.

"No, bring us two portions of noodles," Ottavio says to him. "Not too much. Don't bring us a ton."

"I'll bring you a taste, Excellency," Toni says. He hovers over Ottavio with false solicitude, his jacket crooked, his thick head down; he says, "But you'll ask me for more: wait and see." He remains another moment, he retires.

"And the wine," Ottavio says to him, not raising his voice, when Toni is already almost out of the room.

Lise looks out of the window: the waves of the hills,

black on dark purple on dark blue; the luminous dots of the city scattered below, distant.

A waiter arrives with the wine; he goes through the whole procedure of presenting the bottle to Ottavio and the reading of the label and the nod of approval and the cautious drawing of the cork and pouring of a minimum quantity and the tasting and the second approval and the definitive pouring. Lise observes the movements as if she didn't understand their meaning; as if she were seeing them at a distance of kilometers. She feels lost in space, without equilibrium.

Ottavio raises his glass, says "Cheers."

"Cheers," Lise says, raising hers with nervous fingers. She clicks it against his; a cold drop or two spills and slides over her hand, her wrist. She drinks a long sip, without thinking of the taste.

They remain for a couple of minutes with their glasses in their hands, in search of subjects. Ottavio observes his glass against the light, as if it interested him very much. There are crickets in the garden; voices of other customers seep through a wall.

Ottavio makes a vague gesture to indicate the restaurant, says, "Once I was here with Macno. I believe it was five years ago. We came with the whole *Collisions* team." He takes a sip of wine, looks around; he says, "But even then he loathed restaurants. It's incredible, he's never been able to bear sitting at table for more than half an hour. You've seen at the palace, too, how he suffers every time he's forced into an official dinner or supper. You can't imagine the lengths he'll go to get out of them."

Lise listens to him, and the mere fact that they are

talking about Macno makes her feel less lost, less without equilibrium. She drinks more wine; she feels it begin to circulate in her blood.

Ottavio says, "When you think that, in this city, political relationships have always been cultivated in restaurants, you can imagine the problems this loathing of his has created. All agreements, big decisions, basic contacts have always been established while eating. Eating maybe for hours and hours, from nine in the evening till two in the morning, and drinking to seal the bargain, and then eating again. I realize that to an outsider it could look a bit monstrous, but on the other hand the fundamental flexibility of the national political style is also due to this, and it would be absurd not to bear that in mind. Don't you think?" He looks straight into Lise's eyes.

"Mm," Lise says. Actually she doesn't follow Ottavio's words at length, but glides over them, attracted by the images of Macno that gradually form. She drinks the icy white wine, which is beginning to go to her head.

Ottavio finishes his glass, fills Lise's and then his own. He says, "I mean, the greatest danger for a leader is to seem too enigmatic to his followers, too different from them in little things. A bit of enigma is fine, because it helps create a perspective, but then there must be recognizable elements, features we can compare with those same features in each of us, to convince ourselves that after all we're dealing with a human being. Am I right?"

"Yes," Lise says in a low voice. Now the images are vaguer; her attention flutters further away. The wine expands her thoughts, makes them whirl slowly in her head.

Ottavio finishes his second glass; he says, "In any case, I don't believe there's anything wrong with spending a few hours in a restaurant every now and then, especially if one is lucky enough to have such exquisite company." He smiles, and his features are freer than usual; there is a livelier light in his eyes.

Toni arrives with a platter of yellow noodles; he says, "Here we are." He sets it on a service table, rapidly mixes, distributes in two plates.

"Not a ton, Toni," Ottavio says.

"No, Excellency," Toni says, still serving more. He signals to a waiter, who comes over and holds out to him a little tray with a truffle and a slicer. Toni slices the truffle over the two plates: the aromatic slices glide onto the yellow strips of hot pasta. He sets the plates in front of Lise and Ottavio, then withdraws with his conspirator's smile, says, "Enjoy your meal."

As soon as he has gone, Lise bends over her plate, sniffs it. She says, "It smells disgusting!"

Ottavio laughs: amused and self-confident, elegant in his blue jacket with its Tartar collar. He says, "Well, it's all in the point of view, I imagine."

Lise twirls the noodles around her fork with a cautious movement of her wrist. Her movements are as slow as her thoughts, slowed further by Ottavio's close and unswerving attention. She lifts the noodles to her mouth, tastes them, swallows. She says, "Why, the truffle has no taste at all. It's nothing but smell."

Ottavio laughs again; he says, "It's true. It's mostly smell. And this isn't even their season." He eats without displaying much interest in the food; he fills Lise's glass.

Lise drinks, looks at the window. She thinks of the empty space that separates the restaurant from Macno's palace.

Ottavio says, "Have you been living long in New York?"

"No, a couple of years," Lise says.

"It's a magnificent city," Ottavio says. He takes a sip of wine.

"I don't know," Lise says. "At the beginning I liked it a lot, at least compared to Munich. But now I don't know any more. I have no idea where I'd really like to live."

Ottavio follows her every gesture: the way she bends her head, brushes a lock of hair from her brow with two fingers. He says to her, "It's not easy to find a place that really corresponds to what we are. And maybe it's even more difficult if every possibility is open, the way it is for you, young and free and full of ideas and energy."

"Hm," Lise says, with the shadow of a smile on her lips. Ottavio's attention is communicating to her a subtle vibration of self-satisfaction that begins to be reflected in her movements, her changes of expression, the way she looks at her glass.

Ottavio says, "Actually, I don't believe people are ever completely satisfied with the place where they live. Only fools are. But sometimes a slight adjustment is enough, a minimal adaptation of our demands, and the situation becomes perfect."

Lise finishes the noodles, sets down her fork. The conversation is not really easy, in spite of the wine and the attention.

"Would you live in this city, then?" Ottavio asks her.

Lise takes a sip of wine; she says, "I don't know. I mean, I don't know what it would be like to live here normally. To live in a normal house, outside of Macno's palace. I mean, I don't remember very clearly the month

I was in the pension, but from what I do remember it was another city, practically."

"Oh, of course," Ottavio says. "You're right."

Lise watches him pour some more wine, but now the idea of living in this city, outside of Macno's palace, fills her with alarm, makes her feel lost again and without equilibrium. She casts a panicked glance at the window.

Toni comes back, superintending a waiter who clears away the empty plates. He says, "How was it, Excellency?"

"Nothing special," Ottavio says. "The truffle was frozen and had no flavor, and it all tasted only of that dreadful cream you poured over everything."

Toni assumes a feigned amazement: he shifts his little eyes from Ottavio to the waiter's hands to Ottavio. He says, "But really . . ." He doesn't even bother to apologize much; he says, "What can we bring you, Excellency? Would you like some lamb, some nice kidneys, a baked head of kid? Or some tender sucking pig with a touch of garlic and pepper?"

"What would you like?" Ottavio asks Lise.

"Nothing, I think," Lise says. She glances along the edge of the table. She is stifling now.

Toni says, "There's some very fresh liver, really wonderful; I saw the calf slaughtered myself this morning."

"I'm not hungry, thank you," Lise says, looking at the breadcrumbs scattered over the tablecloth. It seems to her that the distance from the palace is too boundless for her ever to retrace it. She remains very still in her chair, tries not to tilt her head.

Ottavio says to her, "Shall I have them bring you just a salad, or some cheese?"

"I really don't want anything," Lise says, her voice unsteady. "I'm not hungry." Her fingertips are sticky; she glances out of the window and a dizzy feeling comes over her.

"We won't have anything else," Ottavio says to Toni.

"But, Excellency, not even a little lobster?" Toni says. "A few snails in white wine . . ."

"Nothing," Ottavio says. He turns to check on Lise, tries to see her eyes.

Toni backs to the door, disappears.

Ottavio touches Lise's hand lightly; he says, "Is something wrong?"

"No," Lise says. She looks at the cloth, chews her lips. She says, "Maybe I drank too much wine."

"Shall we go outside?" Ottavio says. "You want to leave?"

"Yes," Lise says. She stands up, allows him to take her arm.

They go out, followed to the door by Toni, who bows. They walk around the restaurant in the night air streaked by a thread of breeze. A party of customers is swarming out of three great automobiles: the men fat and noisy, the women clinging to one another's arms and unsteady on their heels, hampered by their dresses, which are tight at the knees. Ottavio stops, waits for them to enter. He holds Lise's arm in the most delicate way, the contact almost erased by the elegance of the attitude. They wait in the shelter of an oak for a minute, but the group lingers, making a racket, on the steps of the entrance; Ottavio rapidly leads Lise to the car, opens her door.

Lise sinks back on the seat, and as soon as the car comes out into the road she feels her equilibrium return.

Ottavio drives carefully around the curves that go downhill; he checks Lise with rapid sidelong glances.

Lise says, "I'm sorry, damn it. Every time I end up making some kind of scene."

"It's my fault," Ottavio says. "I'm the one who always gets things wrong."

"That's not true," Lise says. She looks out the window: the trees and dark bushes flowing past. She says, "Yesterday, too, I felt a real idiot, crying like that."

Ottavio looks at the street, revealed curve after curve by the bright lights; he says, "You've no reason to feel like an idiot."

"Yes, I do," Lise says. She gnaws her thumb; she says, "The fact is, I didn't expect him to be like that. I mean, I expected him to be incredible, but when I saw that tape he was so . . . I don't know how to say it. So rich, so intense, I don't know, so full of extraordinary energy. In a strange way it was as if he were giving you flashes of a different perspective, I don't know, like images that suddenly seem to let you understand everything but they're too brief for you to understand really, but all the same they give you an idea for an instant and you don't know how to express it because you don't know what it is exactly." She looks at Ottavio's hands on the wheel, his blue eyes as he turns for an instant. She says, "Well, anyway, I can't explain myself, not at all."

"No, no," Ottavio says. "On the contrary, you explain yourself very well. And what you say is true. It happened to me, too, to feel a kind of dismay at the ineffability of what Macno succeeded in communicating. At that message that leaped over every filter of articulated thought and went straight to touch the strings we have

217

inside us, to bring flashes of light, the way you said. I believe millions of people have felt the same sensations, in a more or less conscious fashion. And certainly millions of people reacted by crying, the way you did."

Lise looks at his profile, illuminated for a second by the headlights of a car coming up in the opposite direction. She says to him, "Why do you speak in the past tense?"

Ottavio looks ahead; he says, "Well." He shifts gears, looks at the street. He says, "Because he's very different now."

"In what way?" Lise asks him, feeling her anxiety mounting.

Ottavio drives for a few seconds without speaking, concentrating on the beams of the headlights, which sweep the flank of the hill. He says, "You see, Macno has always had this extraordinary power of attraction. It's hard to explain exactly what it consists of, hard to find words to define it. I imagine that in order to define it you'd first have to understand what it consists of: so it's a vicious circle. Anyway, Macno had it at the age of twenty-eight, when I met him; perhaps he already had it when he was a boy. There was something in his movements, in his voice. He had those *eyes*. If he had been born in another country, perhaps he would have gone on being a rock singer: it's hard to say. But sooner or later I believe he would have gone further in any case. Because Macno is one of those characters who have a kind of destiny, to change history. One turns up every century, perhaps. You have no idea of the effect Macno had, the first months, on the spirit of this country, on national attitudes. I mean, everything was so rotten, so deeply corrupt, that nobody who knew the situation at all could hope things would ever really improve. And yet during the first months Macno was in power, it seemed that this country could take another path."

"And then?" Lise asks, looking at the street.

"Then, on the contrary, it was he who changed," Ottavio says. "He went further, and his ideas became impossible to achieve. They simply had no connection with reality any more."

"How?" Lise says.

Ottavio says, "Well, you see, it's one thing to agree that in this country the environment has always been exploited and used as a garbage dump by anybody ready to spend a little money; but it's another thing to think of closing down all the polluting industries overnight. It's one thing to agree that life in the crowded industrial suburbs is inhuman; it's another thing to decide to blow them up with dynamite. Macno won't accept implications. He won't accept time, he won't accept the space between an idea and the reality."

Lise looks at him in profile, concentrating on the sound of his words. The lights of a built-up area flow by, the houses of gray cement overlooking the street.

Ottavio shifts up, his every gesture precise. He says, "You understand: the point is to find an equilibrium between the various interests and who represents them. And since the easiest equilibrium is what already exists, you have to move cautiously, by gradual adjustments, and maybe even go backward, let things settle down. But this is what Macno refuses to understand, or at least to accept. He refuses to accept the fact that governing doesn't mean having big, wonderful ideas and immediately applying them to the world. Governing means having little, flexible ideas, and being able to alter them according to the situation."

The car climbs the ramp to the superhighway; Ottavio turns the wheel with fluid gestures, following the wide curve. He keeps the motor tight; he looks ahead.

Lise says, "But Macno is different. Macno mustn't respect times and equilibriums. He can do without them or change them, invent others. People will follow him anyway, whatever he does." She has an anxious voice now, anxious eyes in the shadow of the car, which starts speeding along the highway.

"I don't think so, Lise," Ottavio says. There is only the faint hum of the air conditioning, the rustle of the sliced wind, the flow of the tires; the low vibration of the engine. Ottavio says, "Of course, so far, every time the situation seemed on the verge of collapse Macno just had to make another speech and stir up everyone's enthusiasm again, sweep them all away and convince them it was worth making some sacrifice in order to go ahead with the great utopia. But it takes more than enthusiasm to keep a country on its feet. And many times I've thought that perhaps the very ease with which Macno attracts and inspires people prevents him from understanding how complicated the mechanisms of power really are. There are so many things he's always taken for granted, as if history had to meet him halfway no matter what."

"What things, for example?" Lise says.

"Everything," Ottavio says. "He's taken for granted the thrilling ease of the whole business. I remember one of the first days, three years ago, he and I and Uto Rumi were in a room on the second floor of the old presidential

220

palace, with all those mirrors and gilt and Persian carpets and chandeliers. Macno was looking out the window with a view of the whole city, and he turned to me and Uto and said: Isn't it incredible? With this look of a little boy amazed by what he's done. He's never realized that it was all possible only because this country was so terribly abandoned to its own devices."

Lise says, "Now look. Macno knows very well what he does. He's one of the most lucid people in existence."

"Of course, he's incredibly lucid," Ottavio says, flashing his bright lights at a little white car, which swerves aside. "But only when he wants to be: this is the problem. When, on the contrary, the developments of reality prove different from what he was hoping, then he turns vague and fatalistic. He begins to say that the only thing that happens is what must happen, that you shouldn't oppose the flow of the situation, et cetera. With the result that the situation in the last two years has only got worse, as soon as the enthusiasm of the early days was used up. The forces that had bet on Macno when he seemed the only way to escape the octopus that was dragging the country into the abyss looked on for a few months, and then they withdrew. Of course, Macno did nothing to reassure them. And popular support, as we know, is fickle: it has to be constantly stirred up. Macno is well aware of the situation, only instead of noting it and becoming more realistic, he's continued going further, until he has completely lost contact."

"In what sense has he lost contact?" Lise says. The car is now speeding at almost two hundred kilometers per hour: the lights of the slower cars flash past, the lights of the outlying districts.

221

Ottavio says, "Macno has never been a politician. He's never had a political program, or a system of public relations, or any capacity for political analysis, incredible as that may seem. He was interested in the world, in life, as he used to say. He had this sort of utopian vision, childish, too, if you like, of how things could be *instead*, of how pleasant our existence could be if we were all different from the way we are, and the environment different from the way it is, and relationships between people and roles, et cetera. And, understandably in the beginning this vision aroused enthusiasm, given Macno's charisma and the situation the country was in, the disgust and hatred people felt for politicians. But between utopia and reality there's an abyss, and when Macno began to realize it, to realize how difficult it is to achieve even a part of what he would like on such a grand scale, then he went away. He became more and more abstract, less and less comprehensible." He looks away from the road to give Lise a rapid glance. He says, "Before he wanted too much, too fast, and that was already trouble; but now he doesn't even know what he wants, and it's a real tragedy."

Lise is silent. She looks out the window as the car slows down and leaves the superhighway along a descending curve toward the city with its little lighted windows.

T W E N T Y - F I V E

Gloria Hedges sips a drink red with grenadine through a long straw; she is seated on a little wicker settee by a window. On her lap she has a pad of paper; she shifts her gaze along the lines, making rapid marks with a pencil. There are two other people in the little room, seated near the entrance. Three large fans spin their blades at the ceiling, stirring the hot air.

Lise hesitates in the doorway for a few seconds; she comes in, says "Hi." She sits on the wicker armchair beside the settee.

"Hi," Gloria Hedges says, looking up. She reaches out

to put the goblet on a table. She says, "How's everything?"

Lise says, "So-so." She chews her lip; she points to the writing pad on Gloria Hedges's lap: the parts crossed out in pencil. She says, "What about your work?"

"Hm, I think I'll end up throwing it all away," Gloria Hedges says. She takes the pad, drops it on the table: the pages fan out, like a deck of huge playing cards, thin and faded. She says, "Even before, I would sometimes get depressed when I reread what I'd written, but not this much. I mean, it never happened that I was *embarrassed* to reread."

"But why?" Lise asks. She is distracted by other thoughts, but also interested: curious at the idea that perhaps her distraction and her interest have the same source.

"I don't know," Gloria Hedges says. She picks up the goblet of grenadine again, sucks on the straw; the red liquid rises, transparent. She makes a nervous gesture with her left hand to indicate the room, the palace, perhaps the whole city. She says, "It's the climate here. There's no way to have even a minimum of lucidity, a minimum of perspective to understand what's being done." She sets down the goblet, in which only some crushed ice is left, with the palest red glint. She says, "I've gone on writing like an idiot all this time, without realizing that I was just making a superficial copy of *Unstable States.* You get the idea?"

"That's strange," Lise says, looking at the sheets of paper on the table.

"I don't know if it's strange," Gloria Hedges says. "I only know that I'm staying here another two days to see the speech, and then back I go to Los Angeles." She shakes her head, says, "Maybe every now and then it's good to lose a bit of self-confidence, but beyond a certain point all it does is destroy you." She sucks up the pale red from the bottom of the goblet.

Lise looks at the fans in the ceiling; she bends back to feel the stirred air on her face. There is only the steady whir of the blades, the murmur of the pair sitting at the other side of the room.

Gloria Hedges sets down the goblet; she slaps the pages a few times to shape them into a neat pile again.

Lise presses with one foot and slides her chair backward; she says, "Is he *always* like this? Macno?"

"How do you mean?" Gloria Hedges says, tilting her head. She also speaks in a low voice, never looking directly at Lise.

"Like this," Lise says. "Does he always have this way of making a person feel like the center of the world and showing how close he is and open and amused and interested, and then he switches off the contact all of a sudden and goes away for good?"

Gloria Hedges looks for a moment into her eyes; she looks at the light that filters through the white curtains and spills over the floor. She says, "I think so. At least as far as I can tell."

"But, I mean, does it happen very often?" Lise says. She looks at the pages on the table, looks at her own nervous hand.

"Every time, I believe," Gloria Hedges says. "Every time he meets a woman who's a bit pretty or interesting, and, as you can imagine, it happens to him fairly often." She bends down, taps her stack of pages a few more times. She says, "But it's not that he does it in the spirit of a seducer. He's not at all a Latin seducer, Macno. Each time he's *really* interested. It's not a way of behaving, as you say. I thought that, too, at the beginning, but he's not like that. He really is near and open and amused and interested, as long as he is. And for a short time you really are at the center of the world." She looks Lise in the eye, she says, "Which is worse, maybe, if you think it over."

They are silent, they stare at different points in the room. The other two people stand up and go out silently, shutting the door. The fans do nothing but create hot currents in the still-hot air; the light is white.

Lise says, "So you're leaving in two days?"

"Yes," Gloria Hedges says. "Sooner or later I had to make up my mind and do it; I can't stay here forever, after all." A wasp that has come in somewhere starts buzzing at a window, slamming against the pane. Gloria Hedges says, "I'm staying to see the speech because it would be a shame to miss it. There's a showing here in the palace the night before it's broadcast. You knew they aren't really live, didn't you?"

"No," Lise says, not thinking much about the speech. "I had no idea."

"Yes, it was taped at least a month and a half ago," Gloria Hedges says. With one hand she brushes away the wasp, which is trying to light on the globlet once full of grenadine. She shakes her head, says, "Which is quite odd, when you think how Macno always wanted to do everything live, how he always hated edited programs. It's really a sign that things are changing."

Lise shifts her position in the chair; she says, "But is

it true that the situation is very difficult? That it's becoming more serious all the time?"

"Yes, I believe it's difficult," Gloria Hedges says. She brushes away the wasp, which is flying over her head. She says, "But, on the other hand, this country is *always* in a difficult situation; it's nothing very new. Everything always seems on the point of collapsing, and instead at the last minute in some strange way things work out. Latin imagination, perhaps. The art of makeshift."

The wasp is buzzing under a curtain, slamming again at the glass of the window. Lise swings her legs over the arm of the chair, sways her feet. Gloria Hedges waves the deck of papers like a fan. She says, "Another serious fault of Macno's is that he doesn't like air conditioning." She smiles, but she doesn't seem particularly amused. The wasp bangs against the pane.

Lise stands up, opens the window to let it out. A gust of hot air takes her breath away and makes her close her eyes, take a few steps backward.

TWENTY-SIX

At ten-thirty in the morning Lise is reading the last pages of *Unstable States* in a deck chair under the pergola, breathing slowly because of the heat. A voice says, "Excuse me" and it is Ester, with a little envelope in her hand. She says, "I believe this is for you" and she hands it to Lise, looks at her for a moment, and goes off. Lise opens the envelope, and the message says: *If you want, come here right away. M.* She rereads it twice, seated across on the white canvas chair: unable to distinguish one sensation from the others. She runs a nervous hand through her hair, goes toward the palace, blinding in the sun.

It is hot also in the corridor, in the anteroom, where two security men salute her with an almost identical gesture and open the door.

Macno is seated at the desk and is writing something, dressed in white in a vaguely nineteenth-century style. He turns, says, "Hi, Lise," and doesn't seem a bit closer or more communicative that he was the last time they met.

"Hi," Lise says to him, trying to control her tone of voice and her smile. It isn't difficult now, and there are three meters between them.

Macno sets down the pen, stands up. He says, "How are you?"

"Oh, fairly well," Lise says. She looks at the window behind him: the park bleached by the light.

Macno says, "Would you feel like going out, in this terrible heat?" He says it as if the idea weren't his; he takes a few nervous steps. He fishes the dark glasses from the desk and slips them on.

"Why, yes," Lise says.

"Let's go, then," Macno says, his gaze already hidden behind the lenses.

They go down; they let themselves be carried by the moving track without saying anything to each other, almost without looking at each other. They listen to the subdued sizzle of the neon tubes. When they are at the end, in the little white room, Lise says, "But isn't it too dangerous, in the daytime like this?"

"No," Macno says in an almost irritated tone. He is much more distant than when they met the last time, actually.

They come out into the alley, into the incredible heat

of the city. They walk along the strip of shadow hugging the walls of the houses, slowed down by the density of the air. From some little workshops come occasional sounds of artisans at work: the shrilling of an electric saw, cadenced blows of a hammer.

They walk along the cobbles in a broader street, and still they say nothing to each other. A man with a tenor voice sings from an open window; a motorbike goes by and leaves behind a wake of burned-oil smell.

Lise says, "I didn't see Palmario." She waves vaguely to indicate the palace behind them.

"He left yesterday," Macno says. Two heavy women are talking at an open door through which a little sitting room can be seen, in semidarkness. Macno says, "You know he's not a real bodyguard; he's a writer?"

"I know," Lise says. "I've even read his book."

Macno looks at her, surprised for a moment; he says "Ah." They cross a street where automobiles, their windows down, proceed very slowly and contribute to the heat with their engines. Macno says, "Maybe the end's a bit sad. But also inevitable, I believe."

"I haven't read that yet," Lise says. "I still have about thirty pages to go." She looks at Macno, but he seems already to have lost interest in the subject. Lise feels a rapid jab of hatred for him: for his way of walking.

They walk under a stone arch. Three men are seated on little wooden chairs outside a bar, with glasses of beer in their hands. They talk in croaking tones; every now and then they rub their bellies.

Macno and Lise turn to the left, into a dead-end street; they walk along the wall of a palace with baroque decorations, whose garden is now reduced to a parking lot.

There is a cement mixer turning; two workmen are lazily pouring sand from a sack into two buckets. They have baseball caps on their heads; they wipe the sweat from their brows.

Macno points to a gate at the end of the street, open onto a green of trees. He says, "I wanted to see this garden. It's been years since I came here."

From a sentrybox just beyond the gate a caretaker looks at them through half-closed eyelids. He isn't wearing a genuine uniform, but a kind of symbolic uniform, which consists of a black, visored cap and a rumpled jacket of gray cotton. He follows Macno and Lise with his eyes as they go by on the gravel, toward an open space with a dead fountain in the center. Two or three young mothers are keeping watch from the shade of a palm tree over their children, playing in full sunshine. One shouts to hers, "Come here before you fry your head!" The child squeals, runs still farther off with the others.

Macno and Lise walk without speaking along a path that climbs toward the thickest part of the garden. The silence between them is as dense as the air: as toilsome as walking. Lise can't understand how she could have run to him the moment she received the message, could have agreed immediately to go out. The sun strikes her head. There is a very young couple hugging in the shade of a carob; every slight swaying movement tends to make them roll down the sloping lawn.

Macno and Lise follow the path, which narrows and enters a zone shaded by thick and untidy vegetation. There is no longer gravel beneath their feet, but only packed earth. Macno looks at a tulip tree with a slanting trunk, largely smothered by ivy. There is an underbrush of tall

231

grass, brambles, and climbing plants of every kind. The trees grow in irregular shapes, pursued and held back and overwhelmed by the wild vegetation. There are dry branches, wild flowers with a sweetish scent, dead logs. Lise turns, and the wild green is all around her, dense and out of control as in a jungle.

Macno says, "I don't know how many other capitals have a botanical garden like this." He stops and looks at an old ilex buried in traveler's-joy: a few branches outstretched to escape toward the light. He says, "It could even be fascinating, if it were deliberate. Couldn't it?"

"Yes," Lise says, narrowing her eyes as they cross a brief patch of sun.

They walk on the tall grass, thrusting aside thorny bramble twigs, trampling on dry branches that crunch beneath their feet. Lizards crawl away, frightened by the noise; blackbirds whir among the foliage at the last moment.

They come out into the open on the crest of a little hill, in a little clearing from which you can see the open space of white gravel at the entrance: the mothers in the shade of the palm, watching their children in the sun.

Macno smiles; he says, "I even tried to tidy it up, three years ago. Ottavio had organized the usual little show for television: Macno who restores the botanical garden in ruins, et cetera." He grazes Lise's arm, points to a shaded area under an old pine. Lise tries to neutralize the sensations from the contact of his fingertips: maintain her perspective. She sits on the grass when he sits down.

Macno says, "It didn't come out too badly, I think. I cut off some dry branches and planted a couple of little new trees, in the right places for the cameras." He lets himself fall backward, resting on his elbows. He says, "Maybe you saw it." He smiles, says, "I believe it's properly catalogued in the tape library."

"No, I didn't see it," Lise says, looking at the grass.

"You didn't?" Macno says, as if he didn't understand exactly what she's talking about.

Lise looks at him obliquely, and is sure of loathing him. She loathes the unpredictable jerks of his attention, the way they fall into cycles and phases already more predictable as a whole. She loathes his being sure of finding her ready to go along with him in his shifts of mood, in his constant approach and moving away. She loathes the idea that he considers her always so alert and willing, patient when he's away and ready to come running the moment he calls her, happy to serve him as spark for a reflection or as audience for a story, as recorder for an idea expressed with elegance. She loathes the natural way he is stretched out on the grass, leaning on one elbow, chewing on a stalk, his eyes hidden by the dark glasses. And she loathes the fragility that at times appears just beneath the surface of his behavior: his seeming suddenly exposed to the instability of time and of sensations.

So when he rolls on his side and puts a hand on her hand, she looks at him and says in the stupidest tone of voice, "Ted and I are going back to New York day after tomorrow."

He looks back at her: frozen on the brink of an expression. Then he withdraws his hand and stands up, and Lise is surprised by the flow of his movements, as if his rising were already contained in his lying down.

TWENTY-SEVEN

Ottavio is driving along a narrow downtown street, between the old walls illuminated by yellow lamps. He says, "I'm glad you came; at least you'll see something of this city."

"Yes," Lise says as he stops and reverses into a free space.

They get out, they walk to the doorway of a large palace with thick walls. Ottavio looks for a name among the few tags by the intercom; he presses a button, says rapidly, "Larici." The lock clicks immediately.

They cross a courtyard with columns, with two rows

of windows looking down into it. As they wait for the elevator, Lise looks at Ottavio in profile; she seems to see him stiffen slightly, raise his chin, make his lock of brown hair fall with a barely more arrogant elegance. He opens the elevator door, smiles at her; he says; "You look remarkably well in gray." And he is close and considerate now, focused on her.

The elevator opens into an entrance hall with a coffered ceiling, tapestries in dark-green shades on the walls. Ottavio leads Lise to one of the windows, points down: the river flowing dark between the whitish embankments.

The hostess is just beyond the door, in a low-cut black dress that reveals strands and strands of pearls over a slack bosom. She allows herself to relax in a smile the moment she sees Ottavio; she gives him her hand, her thin arm swaying. She gives her hand to Lise, stares at her for a second before concentrating again on him. She says, "How wonderful to see you here, Ottavio," in the most hoarse and drawling voice.

Lise goes ahead on her own, moves into the large salon, where guests are talking, standing or seated on chairs and sofas upholstered in green plush. They are of various ages, clustered in little groups that tend to break up and re-form constantly without recognizable rules or motives. Their clothes are much more formal and stiff than those of Macno's guests; the vibration that runs through their movements is slower, interrupted every few minutes by laughter, by crescendos of talk. Everyone's eyes are in motion; gazes plumb the room in many directions. Lise takes a glass of white wine from a tray, drinks a sip, looking around; and it seems to her that the space is full of corners and hard lines that meet, and cluttered with dark furniture, bric-à-brac, and decorations.

Ottavio is at her side, grazes her arm; he whispers into her ear, "Come, I want to introduce you to some people."

They walk side by side on the wooden floor, well-seasoned and waxed. The guests observe them obliquely, following their movements. Every few steps someone comes up to greet Ottavio, shake his hand, and exchange two or three words. Ottavio is polite but hardly available: he returns the greetings, smiles faintly, looks elsewhere. In some cases he introduces Lise, says "Madame Förster." The greeters address her also, bow to her, try to classify her with a few glances.

Lise responds to the greetings, looks at the faces. She follows Ottavio's hints, as he approaches someone or shows her someone at a distance. He points out a flaccid character with thick hair, on a sofa: he says, "The writer Serbato; don't know if you've heard of him. Mina Resinelli, the actress." He returns the greeting of a chinless character with narrow shoulders; when they are a few paces farther on, he says, "Fugnoni, former minister of the economy." He leads her to left and right, turns her around, makes her catch some guests who have turned to observe them. He tells her names, supplies rapid information, makes witty remarks; he picks up a new glass of sparkling white wine from a tray and hands it to her.

Lise follows his indications, looks at the people circling around four or five poles of interest, hesitating between one or another, attracted and repelled and attracted in different directions. And Ottavio is one of the strongest poles: you feel it in the intensity of the looks that accompany him, in the frequent approaches, the waves from a distance. Lise looks at him and is surprised at how different he seems from the image of him that she has had for a long time. It seems to her that she never noticed before the rapid irony in his gaze, the tension of his movements, the authority tinged with impatience as he listens to those speaking to him. She allows herself to be led, flattered by his attention: by the attention of all the guests, which follows every movement at his side.

Then the different swarms of conversation come undone, break up, they start converging toward an adjoining room. Ottavio and Lise observe the emptying from their place near a window, as a girl with curly hair and still-unformed body tries to entertain them with talk about a theater performance. A man in dinner jacket interrupts the girl's words with corrections and explanations that are lost, one after another; he doesn't break off even when Ottavio bends to whisper to Lise, "Are you hungry?"

They go into the other room, against the tide of guests coming out with plates and silver in hand, heading for armchairs or sofas or quiet corners. On a long decorated table are arrayed dishes in elaborate presentations, garnished with carrots and radishes cut in wedges and curls and slices. The hostess hastily directs one of the waiters, shows him how to fill the plates of Ottavio and Lise. She hands them the plates herself, with glances of childish slyness at some little cubes of meat in dark sauce. She says, "We're all outlaws, I fear."

"What is it?" Ottavio says, polite, but not displaying great interest.

"Venison in chocolate sauce," the hostess says in a frivolous voice. She then tries to hold them, speaking with great excitement, making superficial remarks.

Ottavio listens to her for two or three minutes out of politeness, then leads Lise into the big room, where guests are standing and eating with slow forkfuls, or sitting on the arms of chairs stuffing themselves, others are keeping alive conversations interrupted by constant glances at their plates. Pasta is twirled onto forks, bread swabbed to collect sauces; sips and gulps, words from full mouths, fake smiles, glances elsewhere, napkins wiped over greasy lips, fingertips rubbed on white cloths.

Lise tastes a morsel of venison, well done and spicy in its bittersweet sauce. She says to Ottavio, "Why did she talk about it in that coy way?"

"Ah," Ottavio says with a thin smile. "You know that Macno has made all these laws against the killing of wild animals, don't you?" He says this as if he considered faintly pathetic any interest in the life of the deer, and even in cooked deer.

Lise eats the venison and drinks little sips of white wine, and the image of Macno comes into her mind, observing her with a distant air, his gaze hidden behind the dark glasses.

They finish eating and Ottavio is involved in a conversation by two characters with thinning hair. He says to Lise, "Excuse me. Just five minutes," and he lets himself be drawn away toward a window.

Lise walks through the room on her own, drinks more wine, and eats chocolate pralines fished out of a great porcelain dish. Men and women come over to ask her if she likes the wine and if she likes the climate, what she

238

thinks of the city, and how long she's been in the country. They make inelegant witticisms, awkward pirouettes; they laugh and tell anecdotes with many accompanying gestures. Lise replies, surprised and flattered; and little by little she feels her self-confidence flow back, after she seemed to have lost it forever with Macno. Gestures return to her, coy tricks in talking and moving her hands. She speaks without holding back or weighing too long the words of a possible sentence, hesitating over their sound, over the originality of the whole. At a certain point she is again at Ottavio's side, near a marble fireplace, five or six witty and attentive people around them, and she thinks how compressed her way of living has been during this month and a half. She thinks how little she has spoken and how much she has listened, trying to interpret words, reconstruct sentences, working backwards. She drinks more wine and laughs and speaks in the easiest way; she reads in the others' faces the prompt reactions to what she says. She thinks of Macno again, and feels a strange pleasure in seeing the corners and angles of the room, the faces of the noisy and vulgar guests, their movements dominated by superficial impulses that draw them from one spot to another endlessly. She looks at the women with dyed hair who laugh constantly, the well-dressed boys who move their heads to the beat of some bad music, the lamps casting too cold a light, and the general lack of equilibrium condenses her pleasure, tinged only by the faintest streak of regret.

They leave the car and go out into the park of the palace. They walk on the grass wet from the automatic sprinklers. The air is hot and damp; damper all the time as the gray clouds cover the moon. Ottavio says, "Were you bored stiff?"

"No, on the contrary," Lise says.

"Maybe there have been better parties in the course of history," Ottavio says, "but it's not a bad idea every now and then to see that not all the world is like here. Don't you agree?"

"Yes," Lise says, looking up. A drop of water falls on her brow.

"But?" Ottavio says. He looks hard at her profile, says, "What were you thinking just now?"

"Nothing," Lise says. "About how everybody really did nothing but talk about Macno. They kept playing these games of hints and references and ironic remarks." Another drop falls on her head; another.

"Well, that's fairly natural, isn't it?" Ottavio says, pointing to a greenhouse not far off. The rain begins to fall in big warm drops.

Lise says, "Yes, but they were all so hostile." She covers her head with one hand, runs at Ottavio's side toward the greenhouse.

They reach shelter, their clothes and hair already soaked. The rain beats rapidly on the glass panels, runs in streams that distort the light of the nocturnal park. Ottavio looks at Lise; he looks at the palace through the water.

Lise says, "There was this hostility everywhere." The air is dense with perfumes of tropical plants, with resins and nectars in slow transformation.

"That may be true," Ottavio says. "Macno has always

snubbed the social life of the city so much that it's not surprising how his image in those circles isn't extraordinary."

They take a few steps along the great raised tanks in which the plants are growing. The dampness of their hair and clothes is the same moisture which rises between the glass walls, evaporated from the peat beneath their shoes. The rain continues to pour down; there is the flash of lightning, followed by muffled thunder.

"Why do you say he's always snubbed them?" Lise says, looking at the rain flowing down.

"Because that's his way," Ottavio says. He puts his hands in his pockets; he says, "He's never been able to bear this city, but since he has to live here because it's the capital of the country, he's built himself another city for his own use. All the life of the palace is completely sealed off as far as the city is concerned, like a colony on the moon. Which, if you think about it, is just another way of rejecting reality. I mean, does it seem possible to you that a man who should be governing the country lives in his capital and pretends to be somewhere else?"

Lise rests her back against a wooden tub, looks at the great dark leaves in the reflected light. She says, "But has he always been like that?"

"Yes," Ottavio says. "At first I thought he didn't like to attend social functions in the city for fear of seeming too accessible. Which would surely have been a good reason, because when a man wants to create a myth around himself, as he has done, he can't allow himself too much exposure. But when I got to know him better, I saw that wasn't it. The real reason is that he basically doesn't be-

241

long to any environment, and in the end he feels uneasy in any situation that he hasn't constructed around himself."

Lise listens to his voice, charged with irony and bitterness, under the drumming of the rain; she tries to see his eyes, but his profile is dark. She says to him, "What do you mean, he doesn't belong to any environment?"

Ottavio says, "Well, you know that grand seigneur tone of his. That air of having always had everything. But when he came to this city he didn't have a cent, didn't have a house or a car or anything; he went around wearing always the same jacket, which he had bought in a shop selling secondhand American stuff. But he already had that elegant detachment, as if he lived on so little because he wasn't interested in having more. It's that detachment that has always driven everybody crazy. That natural tendency of his not to accept reality and to construct another for his own use. I don't know. With his body he's done the same thing. I once saw a photograph of him as a boy, and he was so thin and frail you would hardly have recognized him. That didn't suit him, either, and he's managed to change himself; he killed himself doing exercises until he became strong. And now he doesn't like to hear it talked about, not even for propaganda. He constructed by himself a way of being, and he succeeded so well that he immediately went further and stopped concerning himself with it, as if he had always been like this and as if it didn't matter to him at all."

There is thunder nearby; the water comes down harder.

Lise breathes in the dampness; she says, "But what is Macno's background?"

"His mother was an Argentinian actress," Ottavio says. "Very beautiful apparently, but she must have had a difficult character. She died when he was, I believe, five. His father was a fairly well-known chemist, who immediately remarried and went to live abroad with his new wife. Macno was left with an aunt, I've been told she was an alcoholic. I don't think he was ever actually abandoned or mistreated, but obviously that is when his character was formed. He developed this orphan syndrome, you see. Alone against the world, without tribe or territory. His attitude toward women, too, is typical of that point of view. He has this almost pathological need to seduce all the women he meets, to feel accepted, and at the same time he doesn't want to let himself be known beyond a certain point for fear that they could also betray him."

Lise looks at the water flowing in streams on the panes; she says nothing. She has an image of Macno running, running uphill under the rain. She tries to think of something else; keep a distance.

Ottavio says, "With friends he's the same, and the result is that he doesn't have any."

"Dunnell is his friend, at least," Lise says.

"A lot of people are devoted to him, if it comes to that," Ottavio says. "In spite of everything there are still a lot. But it's a one-way relationship: how can you call it friendship? On the one hand there are those who adore him and would do anything for him, and on the other there is him, listening as long as he's interested, then shutting off the contact."

The rain falls still more heavily, on the panes of the greenhouse and the grass of the park and the trees and the gravel and the white stucco of the palace. The air outside grows cool, enters the hot, damp greenhouse in fine gusts. Lise says, "But you and he are friends, aren't you? Up to a point, at least?"

"I don't know," Ottavio says. "Objectively, I don't think so, even if there were moments four or five years ago when I did think so. I know *I* was *his* friend for quite a while, but on his side it's hard for me to believe it, in spite of all his usual displays of affection, the ritual hugs and the moving declarations, et cetera. When he likes, he enjoys imagining he is surrounded by friendship and human warmth, but you must never take any initiative, always wait for him to make the move. And every time you fall for it, actually, and you're convinced that you're important for him and close to him. I mean, you fell for it, too, as you well know. And the terrible thing is that, even if you had known from the beginning how things stand, you'd have fallen all the same."

"But I didn't fall for anything," Lise says, on the point of turning weak again.

"Then why do you say it in that tone, if you're so sure?" Ottavio says.

"Because I'm not sure," Lise says without stopping to think. The beat of the drops on the glass slows down; the pouring of the rain lessens.

"I know," Ottavio says. "The fact is that no one can ever be sure of anything with him. He succeeds so well in confusing your powers of judgment, every time."

Now the rain is stopping; the drops on the panes keep

growing fewer. Lise looks at the lights of the palace; she says, "Do you hate Macno?"

Ottavio looks away. He says, "No, I may even have hated him at times, but I don't believe I hate him in general. I don't think so. And at the beginning, naturally, I adored him. He was a kind of myth for me, a person a bit bigger than lifesize. But now, in any case, it's no longer a question of hating him or loving him. It's no longer a personal question, extended as it is, and extendable. At this point the whole country is at stake. It's in the balance, and it can plunge into the abyss or it can take a more moderate course. The question is, what happens if we let things go on like this?"

"What do you mean?" Lise says, surprised by the tension in her voice. The rain has died down to a faint rustle; the moonlight begins to leak through the clouds.

Ottavio turns to her; his eyes shine blue for a moment. He says, "Lise, the other evening when I told you the situation was collapsing, I wasn't exaggerating one bit. If you see Macno's speech tomorrow night you'll realize that yourself."

"Why?" Lise says.

"Because Macno is no longer *here*, he's no longer in control of anything," Ottavio says. "He may be disappointed in this country, as he often is in a person he knows too well, or he may be depressed because he hasn't managed to change things as he wanted, or he may simply have tired of this role, tired of the idea, of his little pseudo-Renaissance court, and the whole business: I don't know. The fact is that the country can't remain left to its own devices the way it is now, to satisfy the whims of an anarchist who, thanks to a paradox of history, should be governing it." Now there is real anger running through his voice, making his words vibrate, one by one.

Lise says, "But why? What's the speech like?"

"The speech is a disaster," Ottavio says. "It should be a celebration, a way of inspiring new trust and enthusiasm, and instead, if it's broadcast the way it is, it will be only the beginning of the breakdown." As he speaks, he presses his hands on the tank of tropical plants, his voice increasingly tense and hard. He says, "But the speech is only a symptom, a signal that things have to change immediately." He comes closer, takes Lise by the arm, says to her, "I don't know if you realize, but this country has always lived on savage feuds and hidden conflicts. It has always been teetering on the edge of the Third World, kept on its feet by other countries for reasons of international politics. When Macno arrived, the Mafia was everywhere, in the government and in the parties, in every sort of activity. And it hasn't disappeared, as he likes to believe. It's still there, they're all still there, just below the surface, and now they're ready to come out again. They're ready to take control of everything again, unless somebody does something first."

"What do you mean?" Lise says, now in a thin voice.

"That we can't stand here and watch while the country goes to pieces," Ottavio says softly, but as if he were shouting. "It's no longer a matter of dealings among gentlemen, damn it. Here we have the responsibility for millions of people. We can't keep on waiting for the moon and ignoring reality in the meantime. We have to accept reality for what it is, no matter what it costs."

"What are you thinking of doing, then?" Lise says.

"Something will have to be done," Ottavio says without looking at her. He says, "We all agree that something has to be done. It's completely inevitable; there are no other solutions. We have the responsibility for millions of people; it isn't just a matter of us."

They are silent, look at each other for an instant, they look through the glass in different directions. The rain by now has dwindled to a few drops tapping on the greenhouse in alternating rhythm. Lise looks out the glass door, breathes in the cooled air. She turns toward Ottavio, and says to him, "Why are you saying these things to me?"

"Because I trust you," he says, holding out his hand toward her. "And because I'm sure you can understand the situation."

Lise allows her hand to be squeezed in his for an instant, then goes out onto the wet grass, takes a few steps, looking at the palace. She tries to breathe deeply but can't; inside herself she feels a kind of vague weakness rising, confusing her thoughts.

TWENTY-EIGHT

In the big projection room people have already taken their seats in the little red chairs facing the screen. Lise goes and sits in the next-to-last row. The people around her are almost all from the official part of the court, plus two or three that Lise has never seen. Uto Rumi, leaning on one elbow, is speaking intensely to a girl with a small head who nods and goes on looking around. Dunnell is seated to one side at the back; he looks at the ceiling in a pensive manner.

Ottavio walks along the aisle between the chairs; he observes those present. He greets Lise with a rapid glance, moves on. Somebody coughs; all speak in low voices. The lights flash, go out; the few people still standing rush to their seats.

The screen comes alight: a child a few years old is seen holding a balloon. The child is in his mother's arms; her makeup and haircut are working-class. The camera dollies slowly, and beside the mother with the child an elderly gentleman appears; a boy with a pimply face; a girl with bizarre eyeglasses; a sturdy man; a very pretty girl looking up eagerly. One after another, dozens of carefully chosen faces appear, looking expectantly; then there is a general view of the huge crowd that has gathered for the speech. And the noise of the big crowd: the confused teeming that swells and swells until on the screen you can see the platform and on the platform Macno appears, dressed in black. The crowd bursts into applause, caught in every nuance by the microphones, spread through the room by the loudspeakers in front of the chairs and beside and behind them. Macno, on the platform, looks to left and right, waits until the sounds die down. The images shift from him to the crowd, and every time they are on the crowd the applause seems to regain intensity. Then Macno holds the microphone to his lips, says, "How are you?" and the ovation swells again, even more expanded and brilliant with sounds, interwoven on various frequencies, hands applauding to overlapping rhythms. The camera lingers still on the crowd: faces and gestures and individual expressions, open mouths, waving hands, flapping handkerchiefs. Macno resumes speaking, walks from one part of the platform to another. But his gaze and his tone of voice are strangely out of tune with the general atmosphere, the intensity of the crowd. And even his fixed movements, his addressing a particular sector, leaning forward slightly, betray a streak of melancholy absent-mindedness. He looks down, and there is a distant light in his eyes. The cutting succeeds only partly in hiding it, with a rapid series of images from various angles that interrupt every movement before its natural end and recompose a rhythm with fragments of ten different rhythms, counterpointing shots of crowd with brief flashes of Macno. Macno talks about the three years that have passed, and the crowd applauds; Macno speaks of time, the cycles of time, in a tone increasingly difficult and distant, and the people continue applauding with the same furious intensity, as if any word of his would produce the same effect. Macno stops at one side of the platform, lowers his voice, and the amplifiers adjust the volume automatically; he says, "I'm not sure we've managed to achieve the millionth part of what we wanted, or have even come close. The fact is that, the more I think about it, the less I manage to understand *what* we wanted exactly." He looks down, and the crowd applauds frantically: all eyes are trained on his, all mouths are open to follow the next movements of his lips.

Lise, seated in the next-to-last row, breathes slowly, absorbed by the nuances of images and sounds. And what at first seemed to her a simple gap in level now seems more and more a horrifying contrast of emotions, which becomes more acute at every new burst of applause. She turns to look at the room: the other people motionless in their places in the semidarkness. She seems to see Macno standing at the rear, leaning against a wall beside Ester, but she is too confused to be sure.

On the screen Macno's speech continues, more and

more convoluted and meditative; without flare-ups or forced tones of voice, with none of the platform mannerisms that Lise saw him use so well in the video of the First Anniversary. No alluring formula is advanced, no adjustment to the collective mood, no simplification or black-and-white contrasting. His movements are still fascinating, but their rhythm is adapted to the rhythm of reflection, to slow, concentric investigations. Then the speech ends; the images shift to the crowd, in a still faster and more broken-up montage, overlapping and compressing and multiplying the images until they create an effect of incredible collective excitement, a fragmented flashing of gestures and looks and movements, voices and sounds of enthusiasm overflowing from the audio and invading the room.

The screen goes blank; the lights come on. The seated people look around for less than a second; they stand up, turn, applaud Macno at the rear of the room. Macno nods, murmurs something without looking at anyone in particular.

Ottavio applauds, standing below the screen. Uto Rumi slaps the palms of his stubby-fingered hands together. Some people shout "Bravo," or "Magnificent." The only ones not applauding are Dunnell, who looks around, disheveled; and Lise, who tries to but can't.

Then Macno starts for the door, and they all converge on him, enveloping him in compliments and congratulations, half-sentences and whole sentences of agreement and admiration. Uto Rumi says, "It's magnificent, Macno. It's your most beautiful speech." He is a few centimeters away from him; he keeps adding adjectives to the other adjectives arriving from every direction. A bald man repeats, "I'm speechless." The girl with the small head says, "There were two or three moments when I almost cried." Others nod; from the edge of the crush, the moment they have a chance, they push ahead, stretch their necks to say "incredible" or "perfect, really perfect."

Lise stands back a few paces to watch, with no idea what to do. She waits till the people begin to leave the room, around and behind Macno, who nods and doesn't listen; she also goes toward the door with embarrassed steps, walks along the corridor in the wake of the meaningless remarks and the empty compliments.

In a little round room there are refreshments. A waiter pours champagne into tall, narrow glasses. They all go to have theirs filled, sip smugly between one word and the next. The conversation unravels into parallel observations, notions repeated with minimal variations by different voices in different parts of the room.

Lise sidles along the walls with her glass. She goes past a window where Dunnell is looking out into the sultry night. She says to him, "How's it going?"

"So-so," Dunnell says. He points outside. "Yesterday's rain didn't help much."

"No," Lise says, looking aside. And Macno is four or five meters from her, in the center of a little group of men who with reassuring gestures are trying to convince him of what they are saying. He raises his eyes to her, smiles at her.

And the smile is so light, and difficult, and temporary, that Lise has to look away to keep her anger from dissolving in an instant, and the disappointment and the distance that she has so carefully cultivated all through these past days.

252

TWENTY-NINE

The air is stifling now. Lise flings aside the sheet, sits up in bed, her mouth dry and her head aching. She looks at the clock on the night table, and it is already nine-thirty. She goes and opens the window: white light enters; the cicadas go on and on in the park, now almost without any colors.

She washes, but not even the water is cold. She dresses, and her anxiety increases to the point where she slips on a cotton dress without even seeing whether it's gray or blue; she slips on a pair of sandals that hurt the last time.

On the ground floor are a few, bewildered people.

There are screens everywhere, in the entrance, at the head of the corridors, in the breakfast rooms. On the screens there are the fleeting images of a quiz show; they are interrupted, a girl announces, "We remind our viewers that the Third Anniversary speech will be broadcast in exactly one hour, on all channels." Then come images of Macno walking along a street in the capital, waving to left and right. Macno facing an enthusiastic crowd, Macno on a beach, Macno visiting the victims of an earthquake, Macno with a hare in his hand in a game preserve, Macno speaking and moving in a dozen different situations. The voice-over sums up the achievements of Macno in the country during these three years, describes the situation before. The tone is curt and convincing, the words chosen with a sense of equilibrium. The rhetoric is not political or ideological; it is advertising rhetoric.

Lise moves from one little room to the next. A girl comes to her with a little envelope, hands it to her. Lise opens it without even looking around: the note says, *Dear Lise, Please don't worry. Everything is under control. Ottavio. P.S. You're an extraordinary woman.* Lise folds it once, twice, presses it in her hand.

She goes along the corridors, but there is no one she can ask anything. She climbs the stairs, knocks at Ted's door: not in. She goes down again, runs into the ballerina from Milan, asks her if she's seen him; she answers no as if she hadn't seen him for some time. Lise asks her if she's seen Dunnell; she hasn't. Lise goes out into the park, comes back inside. She walks from one place to another, in the grip of panic.

She goes down to the gym. The Yugoslav acrobat is working out on the horse; he whirls, sheathed in white

254

tights, as a freckled girl watches. He spins around, makes his outstretched legs describe a circle. His gaze is staring, concentrated on the rhythm. His hands regularly slap the grips at each half-turn: *plap plap plap*, the little blows muffled among the walls, as if they came from a distant depth.

Lise goes into the next room, where there are the rowing machines and the cycling machines and the rest of the equipment. And there is Ted in shorts and t-shirt, lying on the bench of a weights machine. He is pushing a steel bar upward, exhaling violently; he remains motionless for a moment with his arms stiff, lets the bar comes down again, catches his breath. He pushes it up once more, blows.

Lise goes to him, says, "Ted."

"Eech?" Ted says, barely shifting his agonized eyes. He allows the counterweight to win; bends his arms, huffs. He says, "What is it?"

"Nothing," Lise says, looking at his thick sweating neck, the haloes of sweat on his t-shirt. She takes a step sideways, says, "Ted, something serious is happening here. Serious for Macno, I mean." She looks around for some kind of foothold.

"What are you talking about?" Ted says, gasping. He sits up on the bench, says, "What's come over you?"

"I'm sure," Lise says, with even less equilibrium. Now budging Ted from his sloth seems a desperate undertaking. She says, "I'm sure, Ted."

Ted looks at her, silent, with alarmed eyes.

Lise says, "We have to do something. We can't just stay here and watch." Her thoughts are speeding through her head, more and more rapid and less and less clear.

255

Ted says, "Now, look: what should we do, in your opinion? You realize that if what you say is true, interfering could mean risking your life?"

Lise comes close to him; she says, "Ted, I know where Macno is now. We have to warn him. We have to go right away."

"Listen, Lise. Try to use your head," Ted says. He is breathing slowly, even though he is all in a sweat. He says, "Try to use your head."

"I'm going," Lise says. "You can fend for yourself." She takes two steps toward the door; comes back. She says, "Apart from everything else, don't you think that if by any chance we could film what's going on we could sell it even more easily than the interview? Haven't you thought of that?"

Ted stands up, still leaning on the machine with one hand; he says, "But we don't even know where to go."

"I know," Lise says, going back toward the door.

"Wait," Ted says. He crosses the gym; he says, "Wait till I get the camera and put some clothes on, at least."

They run up the stairs. Lise walks back and forth in Ted's room as he slips on a shirt and a pair of slacks. They collect the bag with the tapes, the black bag with the camera; they run downstairs.

On the ground floor the guests move slowly, overcome by the heat. On the screens there are documentary shots: views of cities and natural landscapes with a background of anonymous music. Ted and Lise cross the entrance hall. The guards are motionless at their stations, one eye on the monitors that have been installed for them.

Ted and Lise walk along the white gravel of the driveway to the entrance, they move away from the palace under the violent sun. Ted keeps looking around, clutching the strap of the bag. He says, "You think they're going to let us just go out like this?"

"Of course," Lise says. "Why shouldn't they?" All the same, her heart pounds as they approach the gate. She tries to maintain a nonchalant attitude, and with this heat it's not hard. She looks at the lawn, yellow patches here and there; the bamboo grove near the outside wall.

The guards free the gate, look at Lise and Ted as it opens. Ted says, "Let's go" in a low voice; he clenches the strap.

Then they are in the street, walking alongside the fast traffic. Lise signals to a taxi that drives on. She shouts "bastard!" after it in a shrill voice. They walk for a stretch, on the searing asphalt.

Ted says, "How the hell can you know where Macno is now? How do you know he wasn't there in the palace?"

"I know," Lise says, without looking at him. She hails a second taxi; the taxi stops. They jump in; Lise says, "Take us downtown."

The driver speeds along the street that descends toward the city. Lise and Ted are silent, side by side, sweating on the sticky plastic seat. They breathe the hot air that comes in through the open windows. The driver says, "Half an hour to go, more or less."

"Until what?" Lise asks him. With the hot air, sounds of engines enter, sweetish exhaust fumes.

"The speech, right?" the driver says, trying to see their faces in his little mirror.

"Ah," Lise says. She looks at Ted, who is tapping his thumbnail against his teeth. She tries to imagine the way

257

to Macno's apartment; the time they might take to cover it.

The taxi follows a couple of curves, and the traffic suddenly thickens; it stops in a long line at an intersection. The driver says, "We've had it." He takes a cigarette from his pack, lights it, takes a long drag.

Lise looks outside, bites her lip, says, "Oh God." The taxi advances a few meters; stops again.

Ted says, "We're not going to move again."

The taxi driver looks around slowly, says, "You're Americans."

"No," Lise says, without looking at him. She says, "How much? We'll get out here."

"But we're still a long way off, a long way," the driver says.

"I know, but we'll get out here," Lise says. She says to Ted, "Pay him, go on."

They get out of the taxi, walk through the jam, amid the sounds of horns and shouts from windows and the bluish clouds of burned gasoline, the blackish clouds of diesel smoke. Lise says, "Let's move!" They run along the parapet of a bridge, beside the city buses and the tourist buses and the trucks and the cars and the motorbikes that are trying to move forward in jerks. Someone from an open car window whistles at Lise, shouts after her, "Hey, blondie! Over here!" Ted replies with a vulgar gesture, hurries after her.

In a broad street where the traffic seems to flow, they jump onto a bus an instant before its doors shut. Lise looks beyond the heads of the passengers, through the clouded glass, tries to recognize the route. She says to Ted, "What time is it?" Ted raises his left wrist, says,

"Ten-thirty." Lise looks outside, says, "Oh Christ, we've stopped." The bus proceeds very slowly, stops every few meters. Lise looks at the faces of the other passengers, but they are far from any idea of haste or tension. The men are settled back in their seats or hanging in the limpest way from the straps; their eyes linger on the behinds and bosoms of the standing women, on the thighs of those seated. Some of them cast sticky glances at Lise, who looks back at them with horror, or at the unreceptive Ted, who keeps one hand on the bag with the camera. Lise says, "Let's get off, this bastard isn't moving." She forces her way toward the doors among the sweating people. Ted helps her, a head taller than the other passengers. The passengers move aside, irritated, they say "Ouch!" or "Where do you think you're going?" or "Go screw yourself." They come to the doors, where an Ethiopian girl with a thin neck is standing beside a Dutch or German nun, very pale. Lise presses the bell to request the stop; the door remains closed. The nun turns to look at Lise through eyeglasses with a flimsy frame. A bald character leans down, says, "It only opens at the stops." Other passengers say in low voices, "What's going on?" or "What do they want, anyway?" The bald character mutters a lewd comment; he draws back when he sees Ted look at him. The bus drags on at less than human pace, advancing a few meters every two or three minutes, then stopping again with a sigh of compressed air, jostling the passengers against one another. There is a smell of sweat, of barber's cologne, dead cigarette, talcum powder. The nun breathes slowly, runs a hand over her brow from time to time. Through the dull panes of the door they can see the traffic and the walls of the houses, ancient ruins. Lise keeps turning to take a look at Ted. She tries not to ask him what time it is; she holds out, holds out some more; she asks him. Ted frees his wrist with an effort, says, "Twenty to eleven." Lise doesn't say anything; she looks at the black rubber edge of the door.

The bus advances again with a jerk, stops; the doors open. People pour out, seeking air, scatter along the side-walk. Lise looks around among the people shoving and trying to grope; she finds Ted again. She says to him, "Let's go. Come on!"

They cross the street, turn into a paved alley. Ted pants after her, and says, "Are you sure this is the right way?"

"I think so," Lise says, walking fast in the sandals that hurt.

"What do you mean, you think so?" Ted says, at her side.

"I've only gone there by car," Lise says, looking at the spire of a church that emerges above the rooftops. She says, "But it's this way, I'm sure." She is so filled with anxiety now that it is hard for her to speak. She walks along the walls as if she were running.

They go past an open door and the voice of a television announcer is talking about Macno and the country. They walk on, and from shops and back rooms and second- and third-floor windows the television voice is multiplied to form a single soundtrack that follows them along the narrow streets. Nobody is in sight, except for some dusty cats by a doorway, some cats on the hood of an old car. Lise and Ted walk fast, followed by the undecipherable sounds of the television, from which "Macno" and "country" come every so often. They run, panting and sweating, shirts sticking to their backs, their feet heavy on the uneven paving.

They come out into a wider street, look around; and there's no more traffic. The traffic lights flash pointlessly; an orange bus goes off on the horizon. There are no more sounds of horn or engine or squeals of brakes, or shouts or whistles or calls. There is only the voice of the television, which arrives from every window open onto the wide street, on the small- and medium-sized intersecting and parallel streets. Lise walks two steps ahead of Ted, looking for landmarks. She stops at the edge of a square, looks at two great marble columns, says, "We should be almost there."

"Should?" Ted says in an exasperated tone.

Lise looks around, almost overcome by anxiety. She says, "Yes, yes, this is right. We're almost there."

They walk down a sloping street, turn left: into the street of Macno's apartment. Lise says, "This is it."

There are people gathered a hundred meters away, with uncertain attitudes, between the sidewalks and the center of the street. And just a bit farther on there are police cars and trucks, policemen holding submachine guns, keeping the curious at bay. There is a pungent smell in the air, scattered bluish smoke.

Lise and Ted come forward along the lefthand sidewalk, grazing the closed shops. Lise looks up to the right, and the building of Macno's apartment is gone: the façade has vanished, the walls and ceilings and floors have collapsed to the sidewalk and into the street, which is cluttered with the rubble of brick and plaster and stone and cement, gray and whitish and reddish dust. All that remains are the backs of the rooms of the lower floors, the blue tiles of a bath, bared pipes and conduits.

Lise keeps on walking, unable to connect the images with their meaning. There are no sounds or movements, or particular colors.

Ted sets the bag on the ground, takes out the camera, positions it on his shoulder. He frames the walls of the houses, the street; he comes forward and films the motionless policemen with the guns in their hands. When he is a few meters away, one of them breaks from the group, shouts at him, "What are you doing with that? No photographing here!" He is young and hysterical: his voice is trembling, and the arm supporting the gun is trembling, and his hand is trembling as he tries to reach Ted, who remains out of his range and goes on filming.

Lise is less than two meters away, she watches without saying or doing anything, fascinated by the movements of Ted and the policemen, by their expressions.

And another two or three policemen are suddenly on top of Ted, pushing and shoving him, shouting words distorted by violence. Ted draws back, tries to protect the camera with his chest, shield his head with one arm. He yells, "I'm an American journalist! I'm filming for television!" But the police engulf him from every side even before it's clear they have moved and multiplied; their actions are too frenzied and violent to be legible one at a time. They pull Ted by the hair and by the arms, by the shirt; they threaten him with the butts of their guns; they hit him on the chest and shoulders with the palms of their hands. One or two or three of them wrest the camera from his hands and fling it to the ground, smash it with their boots of reinforced black leather: they crush the thin metal box, shatter the crystals of the lenses, crunch them under their soles, scatter the electronic circuits and the little springs and rotors of the mechanism, the tape that emerges from the broken plastic cassette, and unrolls in curls on the asphalt; they spit on it and spit on Ted, push him and pummel him with even more violence.

Lise comes forward, tries to force her way into the fray, shouts, "Let go of him! Stop!" A couple of policemen turn toward her, shout insults at her, and push her back; one of them, his face clenched, his eyes black and shining, raises the butt of his gun. Lise has the impression that space and the movements that cross it are escaping backward very rapidly.

A voice cuts above the others; an officer comes forward, restrains the arm of the policeman with the raised gun, shouts orders at the others, pushes them back with an effort. Lise looks at him close, but his eyes are as dull and fierce as those of his inferiors, only just a bit more in control of the situation. Ted says to him, "We're American journalists, accredited. . . ."

"Out of here!" the officer shouts at him without even listening. He points to the street with a furious gesture; in crude but comprehensible English he shouts, "Go away, sir! Before I arrest you!" And he shouts again, "Away! away!" waving his right arm violently as Ted lingers to look at the crushed and scattered remains of the camera. The policemen glance after him, ready to let themselves be carried away again by primitive impulses.

Lise takes Ted by the arm, by the torn and sweating fabric of his shirt, and says, "Come, come along."

They walk down the slightly sloping sidewalk, be-

263

neath the eyes of the little group of curious bystanders, who snicker and pat their stomachs. They say nothing; they don't turn to look back. From the windows over their head, television music now arrives, spreading out slowly to form a slow and gummy soundtrack.

They turn the corner; they walk along the deserted streets of the center of the city, under the sun that evaporates the shadows. Lise looks at a wall of stones; she looks at Ted obliquely. She says, "And now what do we do?"

"We leave this lousy country of savages on the first plane we can find," Ted says. He massages his right arm; he says, "That's what we do."

T H I R T Y

The palm trees in front of the airport are sprinkled with dust; the asphalt of the parking lot vibrates imperceptibly with evaporation. There are only two taxis waiting in the miserable shade of the marquee; the drivers, sitting on folding stools, look at a little portable television placed on the sidewalk. A family of American tourists is waiting among a number of suitcases; they make futile signs to the taxi that arrives with Lise and Ted.

Lise and Ted get out, sticky with sweat. The driver counts the money Ted hands him, gets out, not even shutting the door, and goes to watch the little TV of his two colleagues. On the screen, images roll by of the Macno assassination; the curious bystanders, the police gripping their guns, the cars and panel trucks with their flashing blue lights; the house with no façade, the piles of rubble on the sidewalk and all the way to the center of the street. An announcer's voice comments in a staid tone, reduced by the tiny loudspeaker.

Ted slaps the palm of his hand on the automatic doors; the glass panes slide open. Inside, the air conditioning isn't working, the air is even more stifling than outside, saturated with cigarette smoke. Lise and Ted walk on the black rubber of the floor, look around in the confusion of people and baggage. And all the activity they had expected on entering has in reality slowed down until it has almost stopped, in a convergence of movements and gazes, suspended and muted. The same emotions, with few variations, can be read on the faces of the passengers arriving and those departing, the ground attendants and the flight attendants, the bartenders and the porters, the pilots in blue uniforms and the illegal taxi drivers, unshaven, the policemen standing at the doors and beside the customs barriers. Whatever their position in space and their role in the airport, all eyes are magnetized by the screens at either end of the bar and on the check-in counters, at the foot of the columns and near the seats in the embarkation areas, in front of the shops selling trivia and above the conveyor belts circling empty.

Lise looks at a screen, and turns to look at another, and everywhere there is Ottavio speaking, seated at a desk: his face reproduced in slightly different shades of pink. His voice emerges from the loudspeakers in similar nuances of timbre, one dominating the others according to the angle from which they are heard: in sentences that start out clearly articulated and tend to lose definition toward the end. He says, "At this tragic moment, when we suddenly feel so alone before the world. . . ."

A woman holding a baby presses a handkerchief to her nose; a man with narrow shoulders sniffs and stares at the pavement.

Ottavio goes on speaking of Macno and of what he did for the country in these three years; he moves his hands very slightly on the surface of the desk. And for all his great knowledge of communications and his skill in the choice of pace, his timing in expounding concepts and describing moods, his voice is still lacking in color, his gaze devoid of depth. Every now and then he can be seen seeking a more natural expression, in the style of Macno: dropping a word without sustaining it to the end, letting an expression emerge through a little hint of a smile. But his tension is so cold and conscious, his movements so controlled, that the only result is a loss of equilibrium. He realizes it and turns back, withdraws to the refuge of timeworn sentences and timeworn cadences, timeworn attitudes to accompany the cadences. He says, "Macno leaves this country an extraordinary heritage, too great ever to be squandered. . . ."

Ted points to a screen, says in a low voice, "Some tone he's assumed, eh?" Lise doesn't answer; she follows him toward the Pan Am counter.

Ted holds out the tickets to the girl in uniform; the girl has to force herself to look away from the screen at her left. She glances at the names, taps with automatic fingers on the keys of the computer, looks again at Ottavio as the data come up.

Ottavio is saying, "Macno showed us that a desire for a different life is not necessarily a dream of utopia, if we can understand the evolution of history and respect the rhythms of reality. . . ."

The girl in uniform takes a tissue from below the counter, dabs at the corners of her eyes. She tears off the tickets, still looking at the screen, stamps the boarding passes, and hands them to Ted with a sidewise movement. In a faint voice she says, "Baggage?"

"We don't have any," Ted says. "Just a handbag." He points to Lise's shoulder bag, but the attendant is too absorbed by Ottavio. Ted says to Lise, "And thank God we have that." He points to the screen, says, "You realize that the interview with Larici is now worth a pot of money? Wait till Phil sees the evening news. I bet he'll come and meet us at the airport, with his checkbook ready in his pocket."

Lise turns, stares at him with eyes full of anger, lips clenched; she takes off the bag and slams it against his chest; she walks off across the room.

Ted runs after her; he says, "Lise. Hey, Lise." He overtakes her near the show window of a little supermarket full of perfumes and liquor and silk scarves and watches and belts and keyrings. He puts a hand on her shoulder just as Ottavio dissolves from the nearest screen. He says to her, "Lise, come on. What is it now?"

"Leave me alone," Lise says, freeing herself. She tries to turn a hard face to him, but her expression cracks, her lips tremble. She lowers her head, says, "Leave me alone."

"Will you explain what's wrong now?" Ted says to

her, the bag of tapes over his shoulder, his hands out-stretched, palms up.

Lise again tries to evade him; she lets him block her next to a loudspeaker broadcasting music of posthumous celebration. She raises her tear-filled eyes, says shrilly, "How can you think about what your lousy tapes are worth at a moment like this? How can you be so stupid and egotistical, to think about the tapes after what's happened?" Her voice breaks; she looks down, turns to the wall; tears stream down her cheeks. In other parts of the great room, other people are crying: heads are bowed and handkerchiefs are held to noses, fingers brush aside tears. A child is crying in the arms of his mother, who is crying, as the desolate father scratches his head. A group of tourists looks around with mortified wonder. The celebratory music swells, broadcast by all the loudspeakers.

Ted remains a few centimeters from Lise; he says to her, "Now, don't act like this." He reaches out but doesn't dare touch her; he says, "You know I didn't mean to say. . . ."

"Oh, you didn't, eh?" Lise says, in a choked voice. "And what did you mean to say, then? That you're so sorry? That you're sorry but at least we're lucky that we have the tapes? Right?" She tries to look up, but can't; she turns to keep her eyes from being seen.

"You know I'm sorry," Ted says. "I mean, Jesus Christ, it's obvious I'm sorry, after all the time we spent there. But what should I do now, according to you? Certainly it isn't much use to throw fits of despair at this point. I was only trying to look at the business from the one positive side."

"Oh, of course, positive," Lise says, in little breaths

between the tears. The celebratory music is everywhere. Here and there people seated or standing dry their eyes and clear their throats, blow their noses, swallow.

Ted grazes her shoulder with great caution, says, "Listen, that was the kind of game he was playing. I believe he was expecting it, more or less. You, who knew him better, must know. If he had wanted, he had plenty of time to leave."

Lise looks at him, and is surprised to think that through his apparent dullness this perception sooner or later penetrated. She doesn't answer him, but she no longer tries to free herself when he puts his arm around her shoulders. The volume of the celebratory music is decreasing.

Ted says, "Liz, everybody's sorry about this thing, dammit." He turns with her to look at the people standing still and the people beginning to slip away in various directions; the mechanical activities that resume, a little at a time: the luminous signs that, letter after letter and number after number, start forming again on the big boards. Ted looks at the clock; he says, "I think we can go now."

They move toward the customs gates. In the great room, attendants in makeshift uniforms tune the screens to tourist documentaries and quiz programs and animated cartoons, American soap operas dubbed with voices that don't fit the lip movements of the actors, or their expressions. And on the people's faces the moods are already fading: women check their makeup in pocket mirrors; men adjust the knots of their tie; little girls pull up their stockings. Only now and then you can still see a gap in movements, a gaze that lingers in the void; but

270

these are details now lost in the overall picture, brief hesitations of rhythm swept away by the general rhythm.

Lise and Ted pass through the metal detector. Ted collects the bag with the tapes at the other side of the X-ray machine, smiles at the arrogant, distracted policemen. On the chairs of molded plastic, the other travelers look at screens and look at one another, bend to rummage in purses and bags, tap their fingertips on portable keyboards.

Lise and Ted sit near the picture windows that overlook the runway, gaze at the great white planes waiting in broad sunlight. Lise rests an elbow on the chair arm, her forehead in her hand.

Ted cautiously touches her hair; he says, "When we think back a few weeks from now, I'm sure none of this will seem real to us. But now I know it will take a bit of time to get out of the atmosphere." He smiles faintly, tired and sad, but already closer to his own way of being; he says, "A crazy country, this is."

Lise doesn't say anything; the sun comes through the glass and strikes one side of her head. It seems to her that she has no thoughts any more, no distinct sensations. She bends to touch one foot, where the leather of the sandal has almost cut the skin. Then she looks up, says, "And what's that? A kind of conclusion to the whole thing? We dry our tears and begin to see everything in perspective, and when the plane flies over the city we look down and embrace and smile?" She speaks almost without reflecting now; she says, "Is that what we should do? Is it?" Again she feels her expressions breaking down, tears returning to her eyes; she stands up, walks away.

Ted gets up after her, follows her. He says, "Liz, don't start again. It's no use making a tragedy of it. What's happened has happened. Try to be reasonable."

"I'm not reasonable," Lise says, avoiding his hand. "And I know nothing about nothing . . . about nothing." She manages to control herself; she looks back at the travelers, who are following her with their eyes. She takes a few steps; she walks, with unsteady steps, toward the customs barrier.

She looks at the great room; she looks at Ted a few paces away with the bag of tapes over his shoulder; she looks at the planes on the tarmac. She walks on the rubber floor, and suddenly she seems to be facing a choice, without the slightest idea of what it is. It seems to her that she has let herself live in the most opaque way until this moment, as if there had been only one stream to let herself be carried along by. She teeters, tired and frightened and puzzled, dazed by the sounds and images on all sides. Then she is beyond balance and her ideas become defined on their own, while she is in no condition to check them or arrange them by any rule, align them according to points of departure and of arrival and of lateral connections.

A voice over the loudspeaker says, "Passengers on Pan American Flight 450 are kindly requested to proceed to Gate 8 for ground transport by shuttle bus to their carrier."

Lise goes toward Ted as the other travelers begin to stand up, boarding passes in hand, and to collect cases and plastic bags, coagulating into family groups and tour parties and couples. She says to him, "Give me my ticket, Ted. I'm not coming to New York."

Ted looks at her, wide-eyed; he says, "Are you crazy?"

"No," Lise says. Ted's resistance seems so similar to her own that it fills her with anxiety, and the anxiety spills into her gestures. She stretches out her hand, says, "Give me my ticket, please."

Ted says, "Liz, don't be absurd, please. Try to think reasonably. Now, what's got into your head?" He is tired and full of worries; he looks around.

Lise says, "What's got into my head is that I haven't the least desire to say it was interesting but now we return to our lives and everything goes on as before or maybe even a bit better thanks to the one who came to a bad end in this story."

The passengers are now all at the gate; the glass door opens onto the blinding light. The loudspeaker voice says, "Pan American Flight 450, immediate boarding."

Ted says, "Liz, try to be reasonable. Don't be absurd." He tries again to take her by the arm, but she stays out of his reach. He says, "Liz, please, don't act like a child." He is sweating; he no longer knows how to move.

Lise says, "Ted, I'm not coming. Really. If you won't give me my ticket, I'll stay here without it."

"But what are you going to do?" Ted says. "Without any money or anything. Without even a dress. Where the hell will you go?"

"I don't know," Lise says. "I have to see." She is already less agitated now; her heart is slowing down.

The loudspeaker says, "Pan American Flight 450. Immediate boarding." The last passengers hurry, climb after the others onto the bus.

Ted takes the two boarding passes from his pocket,

separates them. He says, "Try to be reasonable. We're missing the plane."

Lise doesn't answer; she looks at the panels of tinted glass and her anxiety disappears little by little. The loudspeaker says, "Pan American Flight 450. Final call." A belated passenger arrives, running.

Ted looks into Lise's eyes; hands her her boarding pass.

Lise bends forward to give him a kiss; she says, "I'm not mad at you. I love you. It's just that I can't come."

Ted takes a few steps back toward the exit, clasps the bag to his side as if it were the only certainty left him. He says, "But what about the interview? Your share?"

"You keep it. I don't want it," Lise says. She sees him hesitate again; she says to him, "Run, or you'll miss the plane."

Ted hesitates another moment: big and flushed and sweating, the fake leather bag over his shoulder, his shirt rumpled and one sleeve torn. Then he turns, runs toward the gate, hands the boarding pass to the impatient stewardess; runs outside.

Lise watches him disappear into the white light. Her head feels giddy as her sadness is transformed into a kind of distant and surprised curiosity.

She goes back to the Pan Am counter, waits while an Argentinian couple finish arguing with the uniformed girl about the quantity of baggage they can take along without paying extra. She watches them, in no hurry, absorbed by their movements, their tones of voice. Then the Argentinians go away; Lise holds out her boarding pass. She says, "I'd like to change my ticket, please."

The uniformed girl looks carefully at the ticket. Her

hair is puffed up under her little blue hat; her eyes are heavily underlined with mascara. She says, "What destination would you like to change it for?"

"I don't know," Lise says. She leans over the counter to read the little words in green on the lighted screen of the computer. She says, "What's the farthest place I can go to for the same price?"

The uniformed girl shakes her head, says "Hmph." She taps rapidly on the keys, waits till the data appear. She looks at Lise with slow eyes; looks at the screen. She says, "Hm, here it gives me Xxxxxxx or Yyyyyy. Otherwise there's Tttttt, but the next flight is tomorrow."

"No," Lise says. She leans forward again to look at the little green words. She says, "I don't know."

The uniformed girl glances sideways, out of patience. A thin character comes up to the counter with a ticket in his hand and a big suitcase.

Lise says, "Which leaves first?"

The uniformed girl glances at the screen; she says, "Xxxxxxx. Two-fifty-nine P.M."

"All right then," Lise says. She follows closely the girl's movements as she taps the data on the keyboard.

The uniformed girl hands her a new boarding pass; she says, "Next time try to think about it beforehand, will you?"

"Thanks," Lise says, and it seems to her she has made a choice easier than most others she has made before now.

She looks around in the big room: the gray and bluish space animated by electronic sounds and little clicks and amplified voices and announcements in many languages, the flow of trolleys and the dragging of suitcases, numbers and luminous signs appearing and disappearing, cigarettes lighted and stubbed out, glasses filled and drained, wrists raised with watches, travel magazines and folders and banknotes unfolded and folded, glances and gestures and handshakes and kisses and smiles, combs run through hair, lipstick applied to lips, shoes laced, children scolded, children petted, plastic chairs occupied in an apparently final way and a moment later abandoned forever.

Lise goes toward the new boarding area, and there is music from the portable stereo of a boy with strong teeth who is doggedly working a little calculator. There is a family of tourists, swollen and sloppy, a family of trim tourists who try to withstand the heat; there are Northern businessmen in shirts with short collars, silent youths with shapeless shoes, women whose faces are covered with many layers of makeup, couples concentrating on themselves, vague couples. There is a young man by the window in a suit of light fabric and an almost white straw hat, very dark glasses, and a stereo headset. Lise follows the lines of his neck, the elegant but firm jaw; the lips that relax in the subtlest way. The man turns and his smile is almost imperceptible and yet it's a smile; his light jacket opens, and on the t-shirt he wears underneath there is written in red letters UNSTABLE STATES. Lise feels a kind of very slow breath rising inside her, a kind of light puff of April wind, and her heart slows down still more, and in the great teeming space where many destinies touch before separating again, sounds and movements become so confused that they lose their original meaning and take on just one, dense and sticky like the air, cadenced to the rhythm that comes from the radio of the boy with strong teeth. Lise bends her head back just a little, breathes on the surface, and knows she is on the edge of an equilibrium that perhaps she will never again happen to reach in life; or at least not in this one.